AGS®

Reading Skills for Life

Level E

AGS®

American Guidance Service, Inc.
Circle Pines, Minnesota 55014-1796
1-800-328-2560

Content Reviewers

The publisher wishes to thank the following educators for their helpful guidance and review during the development process for *Reading Skills for Life.* Their assistance has been invaluable.

Jack Cassidy, Ph.D.
Professor of Education
Texas A&M University
Corpus Christi, Texas

James Johnston
Reading Specialist
Portsmouth High School
Portsmouth, New Hampshire

Alva Webb Jones, Ed.S.
Special Education Consultant
Richmond County Board of Education
Augusta, Georgia

Robin Pence
Reading Specialist
Clay High School
Clay County Schools
Green Cove Springs, FL

Ted Stuff
School Psychologist
Special Education
 Department Chair
McLaughlin High School
Anchorage, Alaska

Development and editorial services provided by Inkwell Publishing Solutions, Inc.

Photo and Illustration Credits

Page 4, © Jeff Greenberg/PhotoEdit; p. 6, © David Young-Wolff/PhotoEdit; pp. 9, 30, 102, 104, 112, 116, Joel Snyder; pp. 13, 14, © Jimmy S. Baca; p. 22, © Charles Mauzy/Corbis; p. 36, © WLS-TV; pp. 39, 170, © AFP/Corbis; pp. 44, 46, 67, 71, 79, 129, 144, 146, Barbara Counsellor of John Edwards, Inc.; p. 52, © AP/Wide World Photos; p. 54, © Bettman/Corbis; p. 86, © Michael Newman/PhotoEdit; p. 94, © Mark Richards/PhotoEdit; p. 97, © Myrleen Ferguson Cate/PhotoEdit; pp. 132, 136, © Corbis; p. 153, © Joseph Sohm/Visions of America/Corbis; p. 155, © Adam Woolfit/Corbis; p. 157, © 1996 PhotoDisc, Inc.; p. 164, © Black Star; p. 166, © Museum of Flight/Corbis; p. 168, © Flip Schulke/Black Star

Publisher's Project Staff

Director, Product Development: Karen Dahlen; Associate Director, Product Development: Teri Mathews; Senior Editor: Patrick Keithahn; Editor: Jody Peterson; Development Assistant: Bev Johnson; Designer and Cover Illustrator: Denise Bunkert; Design Manager: Nancy Condon; Desktop Publishing Specialists: Pegi Cull, Linda Peterson; Desktop Publishing Manager: Lisa Beller; Purchasing Agent: Mary Kaye Kuzma; Executive Director of Marketing: Matt Keller; Marketing Manager: Brian Holl

Printed in the United States of America

ISBN 0-7854-2645-0

Product Number 91740

A 0 9 8 7 6 5 4 3

CONTENTS

◆ Welcome!

Reading is like anything else that matters. In order to be good at it, you have to practice.

Here is how *Reading Skills for Life* will help you become a better reader:

▶ **You will learn the sounds that letters stand for.** Knowing the sounds letters stand for lets you figure out new words by sounding them out.

▶ **You will get to know important words by sight.** Some words can't be sounded out. You just have to remember the way they look. Knowing lots of words by sight is one big key to reading.

▶ **You will know how words can change.** This book will help you see how words change, and what the changes mean.

▶ **You will read better by reading more.** You will read stories about characters who face real-life problems and find solutions. You will also learn some facts about the real world. (Some of these may surprise you!) And you will read about some real people who have done amazing things.

▶ **You will learn about yourself.** Your ideas are important! This book will help you think about what you read. What **you** think about what you read matters. This book gives you plenty of chances to "be the judge."

With a little practice, you'll be reading like a pro in no time! So start reading!

◆ The Five Steps to Learning a Word

1. **Read the word.** Notice its shape. Is it long or short? What letters does it begin with? Does it look like other words you know?

2. **Say the word.** What sounds does it have? Which letters stand for those sounds?

3. **Write the word.** Get a feel for the word by writing it down.

4. **Add the word to your Word Bank.** You will find a Word Bank in the back of this book. It has space for you to write the new words you learn. Your Word Bank lets you keep track of all the words you are learning.

5. **Practice reading the word.** Read the word again and again until you know it.

◆ Tips for Reading Longer Words

Short words are usually simple to read. It's easy to get stumped when you come to longer words. Here are some tips that can help:

▶ **Look for word parts you know.** Is the word made up of a smaller word you know, plus an ending?

▶ **Look for letter patterns you know.** If you know one pattern of letters, like the **ain** in **main,** use it when you come to other words. Knowing **main** can help you read lots of words you may not know, such as **pain, train, stained,** and **raining.**

▶ **Break the word into parts.** Is the word made up of two smaller words that have been put together?

▶ **Look for syllables.** The vowels in a word are a clue to how many syllables it has.

▶ **Think about the sounds the letters stand for.** Look at the letters in the word. What sounds do the letters stand for? Blend all the sounds together to read the word.

◆ Using Context Clues

Sometimes the other words in a sentence give you clues to a word's meaning. Here's an example:

> The **trunk** is locked, and Jim has the car keys.

What does **trunk** mean in this sentence?

    a. the back part of a car

    b. an elephant's nose

    c. a big box for clothes

The words **locked** and **car keys** are context clues. They help you see that here, **trunk** means "the back part of a car."

Look for context clues when you read. You can find them everywhere!

REMEMBER...
If you try one tip for reading a word and it doesn't work, try something else. If all else fails, use a dictionary. Or ask a friend for help.

CHAPTER 1

Letters and Sounds

>
> **TIPS:**
> ▶ Words like **cane** and **fine** have a consonant-vowel-consonant silent **e**, or CVCe pattern.
> ▶ Words like **team** and **meet** have a consonant-vowel-vowel-consonant, or CVVC pattern.

◆ **Directions:** Write the word on the line. Circle the letter or letters that create the long vowel sound in the words below.

1. crate _____   4. coat _____

2. meat _____   5. mute _____

3. crime _____

◆ **Directions:** Here are some more words that have long vowel sounds. Read each word, rewrite it, then circle the letter or letters that make the long vowel sound.

6. trait _____   9. home _____

7. greet _____   10. mule _____

8. life _____

◆ **Directions:** Write each word in the box where it belongs.

tube	kite	boast	lame	feet
mole	cute	lime	treat	great
dime	dome	dame	dune	dean

long *a* sound	long *e* sound	long *i* sound	long *o* sound	long *u* sound
11. _____	14. _____	17. _____	20. _____	23. _____
12. _____	15. _____	18. _____	21. _____	24. _____
13. _____	16. _____	19. _____	22. _____	25. _____

◆ **Directions:** Write the letters on the lines. How many words can you make?

| a | e | i | o | u |

26. c_o_p_e_x

27. h_a_t_e_

28. h_e_a_t

29. m_o_d_e_

30. b_e_a_t

31. m_a_d_d

Story Words

Word Bank

Write each of these story words in the Word Bank at the back of this book.

◆ **Directions:** Read each word to yourself. Then say the word out loud. Write the word on the line. Check the box after each step.

32. orphanage   Read ❑ Say ❑ Write ❑ _____
(or | phan | age)

33. survival (sur | viv | al) Read ❑ Say ❑ Write ❑ _____

34. convict (con | vict)   Read ❑ Say ❑ Write ❑ _____

35. revenge (re | venge)   Read ❑ Say ❑ Write ❑ _____

36. awkward (awk | ward) Read ❑ Say ❑ Write ❑ _____

37. savior (sav | ior)   Read ❑ Say ❑ Write ❑ _____

More Word Work

◆ **Directions:** You can add **ed** to many verbs. Do this to make a verb tell about the past. Circle the correct **ed** word and rewrite it on the line.

38. dip   diped   dipped   _____

39. hire   hired   hird   _____

40. toss   tossed   tosed   _____

41. carry carryed carried   _____

> **TIP:** For words that end in a silent **e,** just add **d.** For words that end in a consonant, you can often double the final letter and then add **ed.** For words that end in **y,** change the **y** to an **i,** then add **ed.**

◆ **Directions:** You can add **ing** to many verbs. Do this to make a verb tell about the present. Circle the correct **ing** word and rewrite it on the line.

42. run   runing   running   _____

43. hurry hurrying hurriing   _____

44. help   helpping helping   _____

45. file   filling   filing   _____

> **TIP:** For words that end in a silent **e,** drop the **e,** then add **ing.** For words that end in a consonant, you can often double the final letter and then add **ing.** For words that end in a **y,** just add **ing.**

Use What You Know

Have you ever known a person who has changed his or her life? What caused the change? Write about it on the lines below. Then read the story of one man's change.

_____

_____

_____

_____

IT'S NEVER TOO LATE, PART 1

For some people, learning to read and write is a breeze. For others, it's not that easy. The Mexican-American poet, Jimmy Santiago Baca, didn't learn to read or write until he was 23 years old. Because of the hard life he lived, school didn't seem important. Then he decided to change his life.

When Baca was a kid, he always felt like an **outsider.** He felt like nobody really loved or wanted him. His mother and father couldn't provide a good home. His grandmother was going blind. He was sent to an orphanage at a young age. He felt like he didn't belong anywhere.

In the orphanage, he decided he needed to be tough. That way nobody could tell how hurt he was inside. Baca never talked about how he was feeling. The outside world would only see how strong he could be. He ran away from the orphanage when he was ten years old and lived on the streets with friends and strangers for a few years.

School was hard for him. Because his life out of school was so difficult, he didn't do any homework and couldn't pay attention in class. His main focus was survival. He worried about how he was going to eat and where he was going to stay. His teachers punished him because his English was poor and because he didn't do his lessons. The other kids teased him or avoided him. Finally, he gave up and **dropped out** in the ninth grade.

Will Baca go back to school to learn to read? Circle your answer.

Yes   No

Then keep reading to find out the answer.

Baca needed money. The only kinds of work he could get were low-paying jobs that no one else wanted to do. He turned to small crimes to make money. It seemed as if he didn't have a choice. He was sad and alone, but he didn't have the skills to express his feelings. He knew he deserved a better life, but what could he expect? His life on the streets was the only life he knew.

His first trip to jail was when he was 17. Life in jail made him worse. He and the other convicts were not treated well. Even though it was a terrible place to be, he did get one good thing. He heard the prisoners read poetry and tell stories to each other. He heard the power of **finely-tuned language.** It was like a song or a sunset. It stirred something deep inside him that had been locked away for a long time. When he listened to another prisoner read, he felt alive.

After he was released, he quickly landed back in jail. He saw that this was how most convicts lived their lives, **like the jail had a revolving door.** He imagined that this was how his life was going to continue. His second trip behind bars began no better than the first. Little did he know that his life was about to change.

One day, Baca got so angry at one of the guards, he decided to get revenge. He reached through the bars and stole a book from the guard's desk. When he later returned to his cell, he opened the book and tried to read. He sounded out the letters. He practiced until he could understand some of the lines. What he had stolen was a book of poetry! As he read the lines over and over again, something electric happened. It was as if his heart and his mind grew wings and began to fly! The beauty of language and of the world broke open for him again. This time he would never trade it for anything. Just a few days later, he wrote his first poem.

Baca knew it would be hard to learn how to read and write well. His reading was slow and awkward. He made up his own way to spell words. But he began to fill up notebooks with his new language. He read everything he could. He begged his jailers to help him go back to school, but they refused. He then refused to work, and they threw him in a locked cell for many years. He continued to teach himself and learned what he could from the supply of books he could find to read. He became serious about his studies.

For Baca, the beauty of language helped him see the beauty of the world. What used to be a dark, ugly, and hard place now held great wonder. Through his writing and reading, Baca began to notice small and good things: the shapes of clouds in a stormy sky, the patterns of sand, or the colors of a sunset.

While he was still in prison, he practiced his new skills. He wrote letters for the other prisoners and read poems and stories to them. Many of them were touched by words the same way he was. They could see he was serious about changing his life, and they respected him for it. The people who worked at the prison saw how Baca was changing. A few of them even helped him get books to read. After serving his long prison term, he was released.

What do you think Baca is like now that he is out of prison? Write what you think on the lines below.

_____

_____

_____

_____

There have been many times in his new life when Baca has had to choose which way to go. Sometimes he gets bored. Anger and hatred get the better of him. But Baca has listened to the beat, tone, and music of words. They are his saviors. Because of them, Baca has not been in jail for many years. He has earned a college degree. His poetry is known all around the country for its powerful images and strong emotions. He has won many awards and has been an inspiration to all kinds of people.

Baca's life story is a perfect example of the saying "It's never too late." As a teenager and a young man, even he thought he was doomed to a life of prison and crime. It took a lot of hard work and faith in himself to turn his life around, but he did it. Today he lives a happy life with his wife and children. He continues to write poetry and other books. Learning to read and write made him a free man. ▶

What Do You Think?

◆ 1. Jimmy Santiago Baca sometimes has to fight off his old ways of thinking and acting. How do you think he does this?

_____

_____

_____

2. Is Baca's story an inspiration to you? Why or why not?

_____

_____

_____

Think About the Story

Use Story Words

◆ **Directions:** Look at your list of story words on page 11. Write a story word on each line

3. Baca felt that words and language were his _____.

4. In the beginning, his reading and writing were

_____.

5. In order to get _____ on the guard, Baca stole a book.

6. An _____ is a home for children who don't live with their parents.

7. Some of the other _____ read poetry and told stories to each other.

8. When he lived on the streets, his main concern was

_____.

How Did They Feel?

◆ **Directions:** Circle the word that best describes how the character in the story felt.

9. How did Baca feel when he was put in the orphanage?

worried   alive   lucky

10. How did Baca feel when he heard poetry read out loud?

worried   alive   lucky

Write Sentences About the Story

◆ **Directions:** Use words from the story to answer these questions.

11. Why did Baca feel so hopeless?

_____

_____

12. How did reading and writing make Baca feel alive again?

_____

_____

Words and Meanings

◆ **Directions:** Think about how the **bold** words are used in the story. Then circle the words that show the meaning of each word or phrase.

13. Finely-tuned language is _____.
   a. words and sounds that are carefully chosen
   b. lyrics to a song
   c. a kind of story

14. When Baca **dropped out** in the ninth grade he _____.
   a. fell down
   b. quit school
   c. got into a fight

15. The words **like the jail had a revolving door** mean _____.
   a. convicts are in and out of jail often
   b. convicts go through revolving doors often
   c. convicts escape from prison

16. When Baca felt like an **outsider,** he felt like _____.
   a. he was out of doors
   b. he didn't belong
   c. he liked nature

Look Ahead

◆ **17.** Do you think Baca's poetry would be soft and polite, or would it be strong and forceful? Write what you think on the lines below. Then read on to find out.

_____

_____

Letters and Sounds

◆ **Directions:** These words have long vowel sounds made with unusual, or **irregular,** combinations of letters. Write the word on the line. Then circle the letters that make the long vowel sound.

1. neigh _____
2. prey _____
3. donkey _____
4. dough _____
5. though _____
6. greyhound _____

◆ **Directions:** These words have long vowel sounds made with **irregular** letter combinations. Read each word. Rewrite it on the line. Then circle the letters that make the long vowel sound.

7. sleigh _____
8. grey _____
9. monkey _____
10. although _____
11. flakey _____

◆ **Directions:** The following words have the vowel-consonant-vowel (VCV) or the vowel-consonant-consonant-vowel (V/CCV) pattern. Write the word on the line. Put a slash between the two syllables of the word.

12. pilot _____
13. planet   plan et
14. matrix   ma
15. machine _____
16. April _____
17. hatred   ha tred
18. program   p_____
19. replace _____
20. trophy   tro phy

> ▶ **TIP:** Many words have more than one **syllable.** A syllable is a section of a word. The word **boy** has one syllable. **Biplane** has two. To show the syllables, you can write the word **bi | plane.**

Story Words

◆ **Directions:** Read each word to yourself. Then say the word out loud. Write the word on the line. Check the box after each step.

21. poverty (pov | er | ty)   Read ❑ Say ❑ Write ❑ _____

22. experience   Read ❑ Say ❑ Write ❑ _____
    (ex | per | i | ence)

23. impression   Read ❑ Say ❑ Write ❑ _____
    (im | pres | sion)

24. duality (du | al | i | ty) Read ❑ Say ❑ Write ❑ _____

25. recipient   Read ❑ Say ❑ Write ❑ _____
    (re | cip | i | ent)

More Word Work

◆ **Directions:** You can add **s** or **es** to many words to show that they mean more than one of something. Words that mean more than one are also called **plurals.** Read the word. Make it plural and write the new word on the line.

26. puppy   _____   30. bush   _____

27. game   _____   31. half   _____

28. shelf   _____   32. country_____

29. branch _____

> **TIP:** To change a word that ends in **f** from single (one thing) to plural (more than one thing), change the **f** to **v** and add **es.**
> To change a word that ends in **y,** change the **y** to **i** and add **es.**

◆ **Directions:** Circle the correct plural ending for each word and write the plural word on the line.

33. self   selfs   (selves)   _____
34. patty   (patties)   pattys   _____
35. fly   (flyes)   (flies)   _____
36. elf   (elves)   (elfs)   _____

Use What You Know

Jimmy Santiago Baca writes poetry to express his thoughts and feelings. Do you have a way to express what you're thinking and feeling? Write about it on the lines below. Then read on to learn more about Baca's poetry.

_____

_____

_____

_____

IT'S NEVER TOO LATE, PART 2

A poet and a painter have a lot in common. Both want to make people feel deeply. Both make pictures. The only difference is that a painter makes pictures with paints. A poet makes pictures with words. How do poets like Baca do this? How do they use words to make us feel and to see things with **fresh eyes?** By looking at Baca's poetry, we can learn a lot about what **inspires** him.

Baca was a troubled young man when he first found poetry. His life had been filled with poverty and hardship. At the age of 18, he found himself in a world where he did not belong, where he did not **fit in.** He was in prison and his future looked bleak. Baca knew that life wasn't supposed to be like this.

He now believes that poetry saved his life. He said it was his "discovery of the possibilities of language that transformed what appeared to be a doomed life."

His poem "Like an Animal" describes how Baca felt while he was locked up in prison. It expresses the fears he had about his future. It is a good example of how poets use language to change feelings into words.

In his poem, Baca doesn't just tell us he is scared. He shows us scary things. He describes bloody fingernails and chalk white scars. He speaks of a part of himself that has died, and of prison walls. As we see these things, perhaps we also feel scared. In addition to pictures, Baca uses sound in his poem. He writes of running those bloody fingernails across his eyes, which are as hard as a blackboard. Think about the sound that would make. The sound of fingernails scraping against a blackboard is a horrible sound. It makes us want to shudder, just as we shudder when we are afraid.

The poet's use of all the senses is important for making pictures with words. A poet writes of the soft clink of ice cubes against a glass. A poet describes the ring of water left on a porch floor when a glass is picked up. A poet tells of the sweet sugar and the tart lemon on the tongue. A poet recalls the smell of roses in the warm, bright air. These words place us on a porch in the summer sunshine drinking lemonade. We see, hear, taste, smell, and feel the experience.

Sense impressions are just one kind of detail found in poetry. Poets like Baca know that the better their description is, the more powerful the image will be. In Baca's poem, "Martin," he describes the first home he and his wife shared:

House furnished with second-hand furniture,
frayed wicker rocking chair,
leaning bookshelves, woolen wall hangings,
wood and wool stitched blinds,
oak wood couch, and phone ringing constantly
you answered to console, comfort, and talk with friends.

In this poem, Baca gives us details that tell us what his life is like. He doesn't live in a shiny, modern house. His house is filled with second-hand furniture. The bookshelves lean. The phone is always ringing because he and his family have many friends. They have friends that they console, comfort, and joke with. These details help to create a clear picture in the reader's mind.

Baca's poem "El Sapo" is about a man who loves life. El Sapo is a big man who works hard and laughs deeply. He uses a coffin for a living room table. He wears a blue baseball cap. His jacket smells like hay. He has worked outdoors all his life. His skin is as tough as a turtle's shell. The details Baca uses to describe El Sapo paint a portrait of this character.

Baca compares El Sapo to a turtle a few times in his poem. In poetry, to compare one thing to another is called a simile or metaphor. The use of metaphor is one of the ways that poets help us to see things in a new way. This is what Baca is doing when he tells us that El Sapo's feet are swollen and have puffy veins. He calls them **turtle feet.** To compare them to a turtle gives us a clearer picture. We see feet so swollen they are rounded like a turtle's feet. We see feet so beaten they are cracked and rough like the skin of a turtle. We see feet so tired they move slowly, just as a turtle moves. We get the feeling that El Sapo is a man who is tired all the way down to his bones. A straight description gives us a picture, but a metaphor makes us want to look again.

What kind of person do you think El Sapo is? Circle your answer.

1. A tiny, fearful man.
2. A large, happy farmer.
3. A stubborn, mean person.

Baca's poem "Into Death Bravely" centers on one metaphor. The character in the poem is the winter season. He never uses the word "winter", but Baca portrays Winter as a soldier carrying a white shield. Winter is powerful and causes great destruction. He laughs a deep, fearless laugh as he breaks the branches of trees. He crushes the world with white. Like many soldiers, Winter dies. However, also like a soldier, he faces death bravely. He does not run away like a dog with his tail between his legs. However, as Spring finally takes over the land, Winter limps off to die.

There is another strange thing about "Into Death Bravely." In the poem, Winter is presented as having at least two features. He is strong and destructive, but he also has a short life. The two things is what poets call "duality." It means that all things and beings have more than one side to them. Life is both happy and sad. People are both weak and strong. Things that are new become old. You will find duality in many poems. Perhaps this is what Baca means when trying to explain the creative process. He says, "Writing is a form of mourning in which you sing happy songs."

Baca is happy to have found poetry. He values words and the worlds they create. In "I Am Offering This Poem," he expresses how meaningful he believes poetry can be. Baca offers the poem to someone he loves. He says it will provide warmth like a coat. The poem will give food like a pot full of yellow corn. If the person is lost, the poem can point out the right direction. No wonder he tells the recipient to treasure the poem. Its powers seem magical. Even though he says the poem is all that he has to offer, he believes it is a wonderful gift. Here are the last lines of the poem:

It's all I have to give,
and all anyone needs to live,
and to go on living inside,
when the world outside
no longer cares if you live or die;
remember,
                    I love you.

Poets like Baca appeal to all our senses: sight, sound, touch, taste, and smell. They use metaphor to explain the new, and to make us understand the old with fresh eyes. They show us the many sides of life. Though poets use words instead of paints, they create pictures. There is another thing that poets and painters have in common. When they move us their works become part of us. A painting or a poem is not just yours or mine. It belongs to the world, to be enjoyed again and again.

What Do You Think?

◆ 1. What did you like best about Jimmy Santiago Baca's poetry? Write what you think on the lines below.

_____

_____

2. Do you think anyone can write poetry? Why or why not? Write your answer on the lines below.

_____

_____

Think About the Story

Use Story Words

◆ **Directions:** Look at your list of story words on page 19. Write the correct story word on each line.

3. Baca's life was filled with _____ and hardship.

4. Poetry allows us to see, hear, taste, smell, and feel an

_____.

5. One detail of poetry is called sense _____.

6. _____ means that all things have more than one side to them.

7. If you receive something, you are the _____.

What Are the Facts?

◆ **Directions:** Write **T** in the blank if the sentences is true and **F** if the sentence is false.

8. _____ Poetry forced Baca into prison.

9. _____ Only people who are specially trained can write poetry.

10. _____ Baca's poetry is famous for its strong images and emotions.

What's the Big Idea?

◆ **Directions:** Which sentence tells what the story is about? Circle it.

11. a. "Crying Poem" is one of Baca's most famous poems.

   b. Baca's poetry is strong in emotion and image and it inspires other people.

   c. Baca had a tough life.

Write Sentences About the Story

◆ **Directions:** Use words from the story to answer these questions.

12. How are painters and poets alike?

_____

_____

_____

13. How do poets like Baca create pictures with words?

_____

_____

_____

Words and Meanings

◆ **Directions:** Think about how the **bold** words are used in the story. Then circle the answer that shows the meaning of each word or phrase.

14. Poets want their readers to see the world with **fresh eyes.** This means they want readers to _____.
    a. rest their eyes
    b. think about the world in new ways
    c. read the poems again and again

15. When Baca was 18 he felt that he did not **fit in.** This means _____.
    a. he felt alone in the world
    b. his clothes were the wrong size
    c. he was not in shape

16. In his poem "El Sapo," Baca describes the farmer as having **turtle feet.** He means the _____.
    a. farmer is wearing turtle slippers
    b. farmer's feet are dry and cracked
    c. farmer's feet are wet

17. To **inspire** someone is to make that person feel _____.
    a. positive and powerful
    b. powerless and negative
    c. mad

Letters and Sounds

◆ **Directions:** Below are words that have long vowel sounds made with **irregular** letter combinations. Read the word. Write it on the line. Then circle the letters that make the long vowel sound.

1. neighborhood _____   4. osprey _____

2. neutral _____   5. seamy _____

3. boastful _____

◆ **Directions:** The vowel sound of the letter **u** in **pupil** is the long **u**. Read the word. Write it on the line. Circle the letters that make the long **u** sound.

6. human _____   8. communicate _____

7. future _____   9. usual _____

◆ **Directions:** The **u** sound in **put** is the same as the **oo** vowel sound in **foot.** Read the word. Write it on the line. Circle the letters that make this vowel sound.

10. book _____   12. soot _____

11. push _____   13. sugar _____

> ▶ **TIP:** Words like **pewte**r and **cuckoo** have the vowel-consonant/
> consonant-vowel, or VC/CV pattern.

◆ **Directions:** The **u** sound in **use** is the same vowel sound as the **oo** in **fool** or the **ew** in **view.** Read the word. Write it on the line. Circle the letters that make this vowel sound.

14. fuse _____   17. duty _____

15. pool _____   18. pewter _____

16. review _____   19. cuckoo _____

◆ **Directions:** These words all have a **u** sound. Write them on the lines beneath the word that has the same **u** sound.

prune football junior loose cookie bugle pudding
igloo unit wooden universe toolbox butcher

pupil	foot	fool
20. _____	23. _____	28. _____
21. _____	24. _____	29. _____
22. _____	25. _____	30. _____
	26. _____	31. _____
	27. _____	32. _____

Story Words

◆ **Directions:** Read each word to yourself. Then say the word out loud. Write the word on the line. Check the box after each step.

33. elements   Read ❑ Say ❑ Write ❑ _____
    (el | e | ments)

34. princess (prin | cess) Read ❑ Say ❑ Write ❑ _____

35. troop   Read ❑ Say ❑ Write ❑ _____

36. saluting (sa | lut | ing) Read ❑ Say ❑ Write ❑ _____

37. courage (cour | age)   Read ❑ Say ❑ Write ❑ _____

38. memories   Read ❑ Say ❑ Write ❑ _____
    (mem | o | ries)

More Word Work

Some words ending in **o** use **es** to become plural.

Example: echo + es = echoes

◆ **Directions:** Add **es** to the following words to make them plural. Write the plural form on the line.

39. potato   potatoes _____

40. domino   dominoes _____

41. veto   vetoes _____

42. hero   heroes _____

43. tomato   tomatoes _____

Use What You Know

The following selection is a play. Shaquana wants to go out with her friends, but her mother wants her to stay home for her grandfather's birthday party. What happens when parents and children have a disagreement? Write what you think on the lines below.

_____

_____

_____

BIRTHDAY PARTY

Time: The Present

Place: The living/dining room of a family home

At curtain, Shaquana, a 14-year-old girl, and her mother are tidying up. Shaquana is dusting an end table. Her mother is setting the dining room table. A big banner hanging over the dining room table reads: "Happy Birthday!"

Shaquana: (Excited.) Guess what, Mom. Guess who just called me?

Mom: Shaquana, I don't feel like games today.

Shaquana: Oh Mom, you're no fun. Moesha just called me.

Mom: Who's Moesha?

Shaquana: Only the most popular girl in school. She asked me to go to the movies with her and her friends.

Mom: That's nice dear. When does she want you to go?

Shaquana: Today.

Mom: Oh, that's too bad. I guess you told her about your grandfather's party.

Shaquana: Well, not exactly.

Mom: No? Well what did you tell her?

Shaquana: I said I'd ask you if I could go, and then I'd call her back.

Mom: Shaquana!

Shaquana: Mom, please! I've been trying to get to know Moesha forever.

Mom: It's your grandfather's 70th birthday.

Shaquana: Grampy won't mind.

Mom: He'll be very let down if you're not here.

Shaquana: I can see him another time.

Mom: (Upset.) I wouldn't be so sure about that.

Shaquana: Of course I can. What are you talking about?

Mom: Nothing. I am not talking about anything because you are not going anywhere with a **crowd** of girls. You are going to your grandfather's party and you will enjoy it.

Shaquana: But Mom!

Mom: Didn't I just tell you what I want you to do?

Shaquana: It's not fair! Grampy would let me go.

Mom: Shaquana! Not one more word. Your father is picking up your grandparents and they'll be here any minute. I want you to call that girl back and tell her you can't go.

Shaquana: Yes, Mother.

Mom: I wrapped the photo album you got Grampy in the blue paper. It's on the table with the other presents.

Shaquana: Thank you.

(Mom exits. Shaquana picks up the phone and dials.)

Shaquana: Hello, Moesha? . . . Hi, it's Shaquana. Listen, I asked my mom if I could go to the movies today, but she said no. I'm sorry, I really wanted to go, but today is my grandfather's birthday and we're having a party for him. My mom is making a big deal out of it. The really stupid thing is that I know my grandfather would let me go. I just bet if he heard me talking right now he'd say get out of here and ask what I'm waiting for . . . oh wow. Moesha, that's it! You call me back in about an hour and ask me again. My grandfather will hear me talking to you and tell me to go. I just know it. Great, I'll talk to you later.

> **Do you think Shaquana's plan will work? Write what you think on the lines below. Then keep reading to find out what takes place.**
>
> _____
>
> _____
>
> _____
>
> _____

(Shaquana hangs up the phone. From off stage we hear the front door open.)

Dad: Hello everybody!

Shaquana: (Calling out.) Mom! They're here.

(Shaquana's father and grandmother enter. They are holding her grandfather by the arms.)

Grandmother: Hello Shaquana, dear. Get him into the chair.

Grandfather: Stop worrying about me. I feel better now.

Mom: (Entering.) Dad? What's wrong?

Grandfather: I'm fine now sweetie. My stomach was just bothering me.

Dad: He was sick in the car.

Grandmother: He was out walking in the rain the other day with no hat. I've told him time and again he can't go out in the elements that way.

Grandfather: James, I'm sorry about your car.

Dad: Don't you worry about it. Can I get you anything?

Grandfather: A glass of water would be nice.

Dad: You've got it.

(He exits.)

Shaquana: (Concerned.) Grampy?

Grandfather: There's my princess. Come over here and give your grampy a kiss.

Shaquana: (Kisses him.) Are you all right?

Grandfather: I am now that I've seen you. Look at that face, **it's a poem.**

(Dad enters with water and some paper towels.)

Dad: Some water for the birthday boy.

Grandfather: Thank you. Why don't you all troop out of here so I can visit with my granddaughter?

Grandmother: Well I guess we can take a hint.

Dad: I'll be outside cleaning up the car.

Mom: Okay dear. Mother, why don't you help me finish icing the cake?

(As they exit.)

Grandmother: Did you use sweet butter like I told you?

Mom: Yes, Mother.

(Shaquana is alone with her grandfather.)

Shaquana: How are you?

Grandfather: I am **dying to find out** what you got me for my birthday.

Shaquana: You want to open it now?

Grandfather: Why not? It's my birthday, isn't it?

(Shaquana brings the gift.)

Grandfather: You open it for me.

Shaquana: (Opens it.) See, it's a photo album.

Grandfather: It's beautiful.

Shaquana: Oh, I guess Mom put these pictures inside. They're photos of you and me.

Grandfather: How nice. Look at this one. You must have been about three years old then.

Shaquana: What am I doing with my hand?

Grandfather: You're saluting me. We used to play soldiers. It was a favorite game of yours. We were like a couple of old war heroes.

Shaquana: I can't believe I can't remember that. I guess you were the general.

Grandfather: Oh no, I was a private. You were the general. You always did like being in charge.

(They laugh.)

Shaquana: Look at this one! This was the first summer I spent with you and Grandma. You taught me to fish. I always cried because I was afraid to put the worm on the hook. But you never laughed at me or got angry. You just put it on for me.

Grandfather: Until one day you got the courage to do it yourself. I never put another worm on a hook again. Not your hook or mine either. You insisted on baiting them all.

(Again they laugh.)

Shaquana: You were always there for me Grampy.

Grandfather: We had fun.

Shaquana: Grampy, is there something wrong with you?

Grandfather: Yes, princess.

Shaquana: But you're going to be all right?

Grandfather: Maybe I will. But it's all right if I'm not, we'll still have each other and all our memories. We have wonderful memories. I wouldn't trade them for all the money in the world.

Shaquana: I wouldn't either.

(The phone rings.)

Shaquana: Oh, that's for me.

(She picks up the phone.)

Shaquana: Hello? Oh, hi Moesha. Gee Moesha, I'd really like to do that but my grandfather is here. It's his birthday. Maybe we can go another time. Goodbye.

Grandfather: What was all that?

Shaquana: My friend Moesha wanted me to go to the movies with her.

Grandfather: Wouldn't you rather spend the day with your friend?

Shaquana: Grampy, how can you compare the movies to spending time with you?

Grandfather: So long as you're sure.

Shaquana: I'm sure. Happy birthday Grampy.

(They look at photos, laugh, and talk as the curtain falls.)

You Be The Judge

◆ 1. Shaquana changed her mind. She decided she would rather stay with her grandfather than go to the movies with friends. Did she make the right decision? Why or why not? Write what you think on the lines below.

_____

_____

_____

_____

Think About the Story

Use Story Words

◆ **Directions:** Look at your list of story words on page 27. Write a story word on each line.

2. Shaquana's grandmother told Grampy not to go out in the _____ without his hat.

3. Shaquana got the _____ to bait her own fishing hook.

4. Shaquana and her grandfather have many good _____.

5. Grampy told the family to _____ out of the living room so he could talk to Shaquana.

6. In the photograph, Shaquana is _____ her grandfather.

7. Grampy likes to say that Shaquana is a _____.

When Did It Happen?

◆ 8. Write a number from 1 to 4 in front of each event to show when it happened.

_____ Shaquana and her grandfather look at pictures.

_____ Shaquana calls Moesha.

_____ Shaquana decides to stay at the party.

_____ Moesha calls Shaquana.

What Were the Facts?

◆ 9. Why does Shaquana decide to stay for her grandfather's birthday party? Circle the reasons.

    a. Her mother told her to stay.

    b. Her grandfather is sick and she might not see him again.

    c. She doesn't like Moesha.

    d. Shaquana remembers how nice her grandfather was to her.

    e. Shaquana doesn't like the movie Moesha wants to see.

Write Sentences About the Story

◆ **Directions:** Use words from the story to answer these questions.

10. Why is Shaquana dusting an end table as the play begins?

_____

_____

11. Why is Shaquana sure that she wants to spend the day with her grandfather after all?

_____

_____

Words and Meanings

◆ **Directions:** Think about how the **bold** words are used in the story. Then circle the words that show the meaning of each word or phrase.

12. Shaquana wants to go to the movies with a **crowd** of girls. Here crowd means _____.

    a. a large number of girls in a tight space

    b. a group of girls

    c. a party

13. When Grampy says that he is **dying to find out** what Shaquana got him for his birthday, he means _____.

    a. he is worried sick that he'll be disappointed

    b. he is eager to see her present

    c. his face is changing colors because of the excitement

14. When her grandfather says Shaquana's face **is a poem,** he means _____.

    a. her face is beautiful, like a poem is beautiful

    b. she has a poem written on her face

    c. her face rhymes

Letters and Sounds

> **TIP:** The consonants **t, h, n, w, g, k, d, c, b,** and **l** can be silent. These silent letters are not pronounced.

◆ **Directions:** The words below begin with a silent consonant. Read the word. Then write it on the line. Circle the silent consonant.

1. know _____   4. knot _____

2. psalm _____   5. gnat _____

3. write _____

◆ **Directions:** The second consonant in the words below is silent. Read the word. Then write it on the line. Circle the silent consonant.

6. ghost _____   8. rhyme _____

7. science _____   9. scene _____

◆ **Directions:** Write the word on the line. Then circle the silent consonant in these words.

10. fasten _____   18. autumn _____

11. reign _____   19. nestle _____

12. debt _____   20. Wednesday _____

13. scepter _____   21. hour _____

14. wring _____   22. corps _____

15. knife _____   23. half _____

16. doubt _____   24. column _____

17. soften _____

> **TIP:** Silent consonants can also appear in the middle or at the end of a word. Examples are the **t** in **often** and the **n** in **condemn.**

Word Bank

Write each of these story words in the Word Bank at the back of this book.

Story Words

◆ **Directions:** Read each word to yourself. Then say the word out loud. Write the word on the line. Check the box after each step.

25. television   Read ❑ Say ❑ Write ❑ _____
    (tel│e│vi│sion)

26. humble (hum│ble)   Read ❑ Say ❑ Write ❑ _____

27. celebrated   Read ❑ Say ❑ Write ❑ _____
    (cel│e│brat│ed)

28. rural (ru│ral)   Read ❑ Say ❑ Write ❑ _____

29. audience   Read ❑ Say ❑ Write ❑ _____
    (au│di│ence)

30. scholarship   Read ❑ Say ❑ Write ❑ _____
    (schol│ar│ship)

More Word Work

To indicate the possession of someone or something, add an apostrophe (') and an **s** to the word.

Example: Sally + 's = *Sally's*   <u>Sally</u> has red hair.
                                  Sally's hair is red.

◆ **Directions:** Make the underlined word possessive. Rewrite each sentence on the line using the possessive.

31. The <u>woman</u> has a green car. _____

32. The <u>dog</u> has a large bone.   _____

33. <u>Tom</u> has an interesting book. _____

▶ **TIP:** Nouns that change their form when they become plural are called **irregular plurals.** To indicate possession for the irregular plurals that end in **s,** add an apostrophe ('). For irregular plurals that do not end in **s,** add an apostrophe (') and an **s.**

◆ **Directions:** Make the irregular plural possessive by adding an apostrophe (') or **'s** to the word. Then write the new word on the line.

34. women   _____

35. elves   _____

36. feet   _____

37. thieves   _____

Use What You Know

This story is about a famous person. There are many famous people in the world. What do you think it would be like to be famous? Write what you think on the lines below.

_____

_____

_____

OPRAH WINFREY

Oprah Winfrey is famous for her acting, her television talk show, and her magazine. However, her life hasn't always been so good. Oprah comes from a background of poverty. As a child, she was moved from family member to family member. Her early life was filled with hardships. In spite of her humble beginnings, Oprah is one of the wealthiest, most celebrated women in the world today.

Oprah was born in rural Mississippi on January 29, 1954. While she was still a baby, her mother left her in the care of her grandmother, Hattie Mae. The church was important to Hattie Mae. Oprah remembers speaking before the members of the church. She was good at telling stories, and she could hold an audience's attention. Oprah was already a big hit at age three. Hattie Mae was very proud. She praised Oprah for her speaking and performing talents. As Oprah grew older, she continued to speak and to act in church plays. Oprah enjoyed being in the spotlight. Church wasn't the only place she performed. One of Oprah's jobs on the family farm was feeding the pigs. If no one was around, Oprah read stories aloud to the animals.

Life on the farm was hard work. The family was poor and there were many daily chores to be done. Oprah's family lived in a very simple house. They did not have all the helpful things we take for granted today. Despite the hard life, Oprah still loved the natural beauty around her.

Hattie Mae was difficult and strict. She expected Oprah to do as she was told without asking questions. Any time Oprah disobeyed, her grandmother would whip her. Oprah was even forced to select the switch for her own punishment. She would be sent into the nearby woods to bring back a strong tree switch for Hattie Mae. Needless to say, Oprah did not enjoy this task at all.

Even though Hattie Mae was strict, she did believe in giving Oprah a good education. By the time Oprah was three, her grandmother had taught her to read and do math. Oprah has always been grateful to her grandmother for teaching her to love books and reading. Oprah enjoys books to this day.

When Oprah was six, she went to Milwaukee to live with her mother, Vernita Lee. It was a big change. In Mississippi she was used to running free on a large farm. In Milwaukee, she found herself in a noisy city where her mother worked as a maid for little pay. Oprah lived with her mother and baby sister in one room. When Oprah started going to a new school, she liked it at first. She was a good student, and her teachers were fond of her. The other students made fun of her for being smart. A few times, the children threatened to beat her up. Each time Oprah had to talk her way out of a fight. But she was always frightened. The older she got, the worse it became.

When Oprah was 14, her teacher, Gene Abrams, took an interest in her. He noticed that she was often alone and tried to help her. Because Oprah was such a good student, Mr. Abrams was able to get her a scholarship to a private school. Once again, she had a big change in her life. Oprah was now the only African-American student in an all-white school. She didn't let this bother her though, and she made many friends. Still, there were a few problems. The school was far from where she lived. Oprah had to travel a long way to get there. Also, most of her new friends came from rich families. They didn't understand that Oprah didn't have a lot of money. In her desire to fit in, she began to steal from her mother. She went so far as to fake home robberies to cover her thefts. This caused so much conflict at home that Oprah began to run away from home.

After a while, Oprah's mother couldn't handle her anymore. She decided to put Oprah in a home for girls. Oprah was very scared. She couldn't believe the bad turn her life was taking. It was a stroke of luck for Oprah that the home was full. Her mother was told to bring her back in two weeks. However, Vernita was fed up. She was a single mother and at her **wit's end.** She couldn't wait another two weeks. She called Oprah's father.

Do you think Oprah's father will take her in? Write what you think on the lines below. Then keep reading to find out what takes place.

_____

_____

_____

_____

Vernon Winfrey and his wife Zelma were happy to have Oprah come live with them. She went to Tennessee to live with her father and stepmother in Nashville. She lived with them for over seven years. Oprah knew this was a chance she didn't want to ruin. Her parents' rules were strict, but she now knew what to expect. Like her grandmother, Oprah's father made her go to church. He had a long list of rules for her to obey. She was expected to behave like a lady and was not allowed to wear tight clothes or heavy makeup. Most importantly, she was expected to get good grades at school. Her stepmother made her read books and report on them every two weeks.

The good home and strict rules had a great impact on Oprah. She became an excellent student once more. She got involved in drama classes and was elected president of her school's student council. Oprah also began to participate in beauty contests. In the Elks Club beauty contest, she won a four-year scholarship to Tennessee State University.

Oprah landed a part-time job at a local radio station while she was still in high school. She had gone to the radio station to collect money for a charity. The man at the radio station took a liking to her voice. It had a nice quality that made her sound warm and interesting. He asked Oprah to record her voice on a tape. Everyone at the station loved the tape. Afterwards, Oprah was given a job reading news reports after school and on the weekends.

Oprah knew that fulfilling her dreams would take a lot of focus and hard work. In fact, she decided to break up with her high school boyfriend. She knew she would be very busy and did not want to **string him along.**

After Oprah started college, another big break came her way. In 1973, a television station offered her a job. She became the first woman and the first African-American newscaster in Nashville. Throughout this period, Oprah lived with her father and stepmother. Even though she was a television reporter, she still had to be home early. Soon it was time to step out on her own. In 1976, when she was offered a job with a television station in Baltimore, she jumped at the chance. Oprah was finally a young woman on her own.

In the mid-1980s, Oprah started her own national talk show. Later, she became both the producer and owner of the show. Even though much daytime television was poor, Oprah did not follow the trend. Instead, she made shows she thought audiences would like. Her ideas paid off, as people loved the show.

Oprah left behind a life of poverty to become a wealthy, successful woman. As she got older, Oprah soared on the wings of common sense and dreams. Her love of reading, her self-discipline, and hard work have taken Oprah far and made her life rewarding.

You Be the Judge

◆ 1. Oprah says that her father and stepmother were very strict. They made her study hard and be self-disciplined. Do you think this has helped Oprah to be successful? Why or why not? Write what you think on the lines below.

_____

_____

_____

Think About the Story

Use Story Words

◆ **Directions:** Look at your list of story words on page 35. Write a story word on each line.

2. Oprah's grandmother was a _____ woman.

3. Today Oprah is the host of a _____ talk show.

4. As a child, Oprah so loved the spotlight that she read to an _____ of farm animals.

5. In high school Oprah won a _____.

6. She was born in _____ Mississippi.

7. Oprah is a wealthy and _____ woman.

When Did It Happen?

◆ 8. Write a number from 1 to 4 in front of each event to show when it happened.

_____ Oprah got a part-time job on the radio.

_____ Oprah told stories at church.

_____ Oprah got a job on television.

_____ Oprah moved to Milwaukee to live with her mother.

What Are the Facts?

◆ **Directions:** Circle the statements that are facts.

9. Why did Oprah's mother send her to live with her father?

   a. Oprah's health was poor and she needed a warmer climate.

   b. The home for girls was full.

   c. Her mother's house was too small and crowded.

   d. Her mother couldn't handle Oprah anymore.

Write Sentences About the Story

◆ **Directions:** Use words from the story to answer these questions.

10. Why was moving from rural Mississippi to Milwaukee a big change for Oprah?

_____

_____

11. Why was Oprah's daytime talk show successful?

_____

_____

Words and Meanings

◆ **Directions:** Think about how the **bold** words are used in the story. Then circle the words that show the meaning of each word or phrase.

12. Oprah broke up with her boyfriend because she didn't want to **string him along.** This means she didn't _____.
    a. want to tie his hands
    b. like him following her around
    c. want to make him wait a long time and be disappointed later

13. Oprah was sent to live with her father because her mother was at her **wit's end.** This means her mother _____.
    a. was out of ideas for dealing with her daughter
    b. was careless
    c. had run out of funny things to say

Why Did It Happen?

◆ **Directions:** Draw a line from each story event to the reason it happened.

What Happened	Why
14. Oprah got a job at a radio station.	○ She taught her to read.
15. Oprah is grateful to her grandmother.	○ The man at the radio station liked her voice.
16. Oprah stole from her mother.	○ She wanted to fit in with her rich friends.

Letters and Sounds

◆ **Directions:** These words have a **silent p.** Read the words. Write them on the lines.

1. receipt _____   3. corps _____

2. raspberry _____

◆ **Directions:** These words have the **VC/CCV** pattern. Read the words. Write them on the lines.

4. crumble _____   6. griddle _____

5. hundred _____

> ▶ **TIP:** Words that end in **le** often form the **VC/CCV** pattern.

◆ **Directions:** Write the words below on the lines and then divide them into syllables.

7. stumble _____   13. unskilled _____

8. riddle _____   14. straddle _____

9. haggle _____   15. purple _____

10. jumble _____   16. sample _____

11. teamster _____   17. humble _____

12. wiggle _____   18. bubble _____

◆ **Directions:** Write the letters on the lines. See how many words you can make.

| c | f | g | gr | h | m | n | p | qu | s |

19. _____ uddle   27. _____ ibble

20. _____ uddle   28. _____ ibble

21. _____ uddle   29. _____ iddle

22. _____ uddle   30. _____ iddle

                     31. _____ iddle

23. _____ umble   32. _____ imple

24. _____ umble   33. _____ imple

25. _____ umble   34. _____ amble

26. _____ umble   35. _____ iggle

Story Words

Word Bank

Write each of these story words in the Word Bank at the back of this book.

◆ **Directions:** Read each word to yourself. Then say the word out loud. Write the word on the line. Check the box after each step.

36. admire (ad | mire)   Read ❑ Say ❑ Write ❑ _____

37. assignment   Read ❑ Say ❑ Write ❑ _____
   (as | sign | ment)

38. emulate (em | u | late) Read ❑ Say ❑ Write ❑ _____

39. tomorrow   Read ❑ Say ❑ Write ❑ _____
   (to | mor | row)

40. ballet (bal | let)   Read ❑ Say ❑ Write ❑ _____

41. library (li | brar | y)   Read ❑ Say ❑ Write ❑ _____

More Word Work

◆ **Directions:** The suffixes **er, or, ar,** and **ist** are found at the end of nouns that refer to people. Write the words below on the lines and circle the **er, or, ar,** or **ist** suffixes in the words.

42. worker _____   **45.** actor _____

43. scholar _____   **46.** teacher _____

44. cyclist _____   **47.** dentist _____

▶ **TIP:** The suffixes **er, or, ar,** and **ist** mean **one who does** or **one who is.**

◆ **Directions:** Add **er, or, ar,** or **ist** to the word parts below. Then write the word you have made.

48. help   + _____ = _____

49. harp   + _____ = _____

50. li   + _____ = _____

51. auth   + _____ = _____

Use What You Know

Role models inspire us to reach our goals. Who are your role models? Why do you admire them? Write what you think on the lines below.

_____

_____

ROLE MODELS

A group of yellow buses lined up in front of the school building. Students laughed and shouted good-bye to each other. They were loud and having fun and there was an extra, "thank-goodness-it's-Friday" energy in the air. But Carol was quiet. Her best friend Antonio asked, "Who are you going to write about?"

"I don't know," sighed Carol as she thought back to her English class that afternoon. She remembered Mr. Suzuki standing in front of the blackboard. He said, "Listen up, I have a very special assignment for you. This weekend I want you to write about three people. They should be people you admire. People you would like to emulate. Who knows what the word emulate means?"

As usual, Tommy Hernandez raised his hand high in the air. He waved it wildly. Mr. Suzuki smiled and said, "Yes, Tommy."

"To emulate someone means you want to be just like that person."

The bell rang. Students grabbed their books and jumped up from their desks. "Wait a second," said Mr. Suzuki. "I won't tell you whom to write about. But please, I don't want to get thirty papers about the same three athletes or movie actors. Consider your choices carefully."

"Cool choice," squealed Kim Reynolds. She and Maria Chun were standing by the school's front steps.

Maria said, "Sandy Starr is my favorite. Mr. Suzuki said he didn't want us to write about movie stars, but he didn't say anything about fashion models." The two girls laughed and ran past Carol and Antonio.

Carol looked around. Many of her classmates were nearby. They all seemed to be talking about the assignment. Some were writing about sports stars or movie actors. Others were writing about singers or models. It seemed to Carol that no one had listened to Mr. Suzuki's instructions.

Chris Fisher ran up to Carol and Antonio. "Hi guys. Antonio, do you want to play ball with us tomorrow?"

"I can't," said Antonio. "I've got Big Brothers. We're taking the kids to the petting zoo."

"Tell them you got sick."

"I can't lie to them, Chris."

"Just **skip** it then."

"Stop **putting him on the spot,** Chris," Carol jumped in.

Antonio said, "The kids have been looking forward to this for a long time. I promised that I would go."

As he ran to get his bus, Chris called out, "You're going to miss a great game."

Carol said good-bye to Antonio. She got on the bus and took a seat. She looked out the window and saw Antonio jumping up and down. He was making funny faces. Despite her worries about the homework, Carol laughed. Antonio always knew how to cheer her up.

When Carol got home, the house smelled great. She followed her nose to the kitchen. Her mother was cooking soups and good, thick stews. It looked like she was planning to feed an army.

"Hi, Mom."

"Hi, sweetie."

"What's all the food for?"

"My psychology exam is on Monday. I want to spend a lot of time studying this weekend. So I thought I'd make everything today."

Carol asked, "Does this mean I have to miss my dance class tomorrow morning?"

"Absolutely not!" said Mom. "What if a talent scout comes to class tomorrow and you're not there? I won't have you miss out on that." She smiled at Carol.

Carol watched her mom cook and told her about her day. She asked her mother who she should write about.

"Why don't you write about someone you know?"

"Like who?"

"Who was the last person you talked to at school today?"

"Antonio. You think I should write about Antonio?"

"What do you think of him?"

"He's my best friend. I think he's great, he always wants to help people. He gets involved in programs like Big Brothers and recycling. He's really caring. He's a good person."

"It sounds to me like Antonio is someone you admire."

"I can't believe I didn't think of him. Thanks, Mom, I'm going up to my room to start writing."

The next morning, Carol went to dance class. Ms. King, the teacher, called out, "And bend your knees, one, two, three, four. And straighten your knees, one, two, three, four."

Babette Miller was standing next to Carol. "Psst," she whispered. "Ms. King is going to hand out parts for the recital today. It's so exciting, I just know I'm going to get the role of the princess."

"How do you know that?" asked Carol.

"Well she has to give the lead to a good dancer. And the princess should be beautiful. So who else can she give it to? Certainly not the new girl," Babette giggled.

Carol looked at Kia, the new girl. Carol thought she was a good dancer. But she **looked like a pole.** She wore shorts instead of a leotard and sneakers instead of ballet slippers. Her hair was always a mess and falling out of its clip. Babette, in her pink leotard and slippers, looked more like a princess.

Ms. King called out, "No talking." Carol was glad the teacher had told them to be quiet. She didn't like talking to Babette.

After class Ms. King announced the roles for the recital. She said, "The princess will be Kia."

Everyone got quiet. Then Babette put on a fake smile and started clapping. Everyone else started clapping, too. Carol looked at Kia, and watched her shy smile get bigger and bigger. "Why, she really is pretty," thought Carol.

On the ride home Carol was quiet. She thought about Ms. King. It was nice that she had given the new girl a chance. Ms. King always did things like that. When you didn't understand a dance, she always said the right thing to help you. And she never yelled at anyone. Ms. King is a good teacher and a nice person. "I admire her," thought Carol.

Suddenly Carol sat up straight in her seat. "Mom, I just thought of another person to write about!"

On Sunday morning the first thing Carol thought about was her paper for English class. She needed to write about one more person. Carol thought and thought. Finally she decided to write about a famous woman scientist. But she had to go to the library to do some research. Her mom didn't want to put off studying, but she said she would take Carol to the library.

When they got back home they heard the phone ringing. Carol's mother ran to answer it. She heard her mom say, "I'll be right there."

"What's wrong?" asked Carol.

"Your Great-Aunt Sarah broke her arm. I have to pick her up at the hospital and take her home. I'm going to go visit with her for a while."

"Mom, what about your test?"

Carol's mother sighed, "I'll take my textbook. Maybe I'll get a chance to study."

She kissed Carol and walked out the door. Carol watched her from the window. She saw her mom push away the branches of a tree they hadn't gotten around to trimming yet. Her mother got in the car and sat still for a moment, and then she drove off. "She looks tired," thought Carol as she picked up her notebook to begin her homework. She started writing about the woman scientist, but she couldn't think. She kept thinking about her mom. Suddenly, Carol crossed out what she had written. She started over. This is what she wrote:

> The person I most admire is my mother. I don't know anyone who works harder. She works all day long in an office. Then she goes to school at night. Yet she still manages to keep the house and our clothes clean, and to cook our meals. My mom didn't finish college because she had to take care of me when I was a baby. I am glad she is going back to school now. She is doing it for herself because she likes to learn and wants to get an interesting job. But she is also doing it for us. She wants me to have a better future. My mom is a good person. She is the best person I know. I love her.

Carol read what she had just written. She liked it. She decided to show it to her mother when she got home. "No," Carol changed her mind. "I'll show it to her tomorrow, after she's taken her test."

You Be The Judge

◆ 1. Carol was surprised to realize how much she admired the people closest to her. Do you think most people fully appreciate their family and friends? Why or why not? Write what you think on the lines below.

_____

_____

_____

_____

Think About the Story

Use Story Words

◆ **Directions:** Look at your list of story words on page 43. Write a story word on each line.

2. In dance class Carol wore _____ slippers.

3. Carol went to the _____ to do research.

4. Many students _____ athletes and movie actors.

5. To _____ someone is to be just like that person.

6. The homework _____ was to write about a role model.

7. Carol worried she would miss her dance class _____.

When Did It Happen?

◆ 8. Write a number from 1 to 5 in front of each event to show when it happened.

_____ Chris asked Antonio to play ball with him.

_____ Mr. Suzuki told the class to write about three people they admire.

_____ Carol's mom left to take care of a sick aunt.

_____ Kia was given the role of the princess.

_____ Carol decided to write about her mother.

Write Sentences About the Story

◆ **Directions:** Use words from the story to answer these questions.

9. What did Mr. Suzuki hope his students would not do for their writing assignment?

_____

_____

10. Who teaches Carol's dance class?

_____

_____

11. Why did Carol's mom make enough food to feed an army?

_____

_____

12. For which group does Antonio do volunteer work?

_____

_____

Words and Meanings

◆ **Directions:** Think about how the **bold** words are used in the story. Then circle the words that show the meaning of each word or phrase.

13. When Chris tells Antonio to **skip** Big Brothers, he means Antonio should _____.
    a. hop up and down at Big Brothers
    b. not go to Big Brothers
    c. throw Big Brothers away

14. When Carol tells Chris he is **putting Antonio on the spot,** she means Chris is _____.
    a. putting spots on Antonio's face
    b. moving Antonio to a spot on the ground
    c. putting pressure on Antonio

15. When Carol says Kia **looks like a pole,** she means Kia _____.
    a. is very thin
    b. reaches from the floor to the ceiling
    c. is in the way

Letters and Sounds

◆ **Directions:** The letter **c** can sound like a **k,** as in the word **can.** It can also sound like an **s,** as in the word **city.** Read the words out loud. Write a **k** or an **s** after the word to tell which sound it begins with.

1. coop _____
2. circus _____
3. cook _____
4. cemetery _____
5. cite _____

6. college _____
7. ceiling _____
8. care _____
9. cement _____
10. clean _____

> **TIP:** When a **c** makes a **k** sound it is called a **hard c.** When a **c** makes an **s** sound it is called a **soft c.**

◆ **Directions:** A **hard** or **soft c** can also occur at or near the end of a word. Write a **k** or **s** to tell which sound appears at the end of these words.

11. rice _____
12. force _____
13. circle _____
14. spice _____
15. trick _____

16. significant _____
17. pierce _____
18. mosaic _____
19. rice _____
20. price _____

◆ **Directions:** These words have a **VC/CCCV** pattern. Write the word on the line and divide it into syllables.

21. construct _____
22. subscribe _____
23. enthrall _____
24. instruct _____
25. unscramble _____

26. enthrone _____
27. prescribe _____
28. instrument _____
29. constrict _____

Word Bank

Write each of these story words in the Word Bank at the back of this book.

Story Words

◆ **Directions:** Read each word to yourself. Then say the word out loud. Write the word on the line. Check the box after each step.

30. baseball (base | ball)   Read ❑ Say ❑ Write ❑   _____

31. league   Read ❑ Say ❑ Write ❑   _____

32. improve (im | prove)   Read ❑ Say ❑ Write ❑   _____

33. athlete (ath | lete)   Read ❑ Say ❑ Write ❑   _____

34. disabled (dis | a | bled)   Read ❑ Say ❑ Write ❑   _____

35. inspired (in | spired)   Read ❑ Say ❑ Write ❑   _____

More Word Work

◆ **Directions:** The letters **pre, re, in,** and **im** form prefixes at the beginning of many words. Circle the correct word for each prefix. Then write the word.

36. im (press / take)   _____

37. pre (please / pare)   _____

38. in (done / direct)   _____

39. re (union / pare)   _____

40. pre (tend / go)   _____

▶ **TIP:** The prefix **non** means **not.**

◆ **Directions:** The letters **dis, de, un,** and **non** also form prefixes at the beginning of many words. Circle the correct word for each prefix. Then write the word.

41. non (descript / good)   _____

42. dis (here / appear)   _____

43. un (often / usual)   _____

44. de (fool / sign)   _____

45. dis (look / ease)   _____

Use What You Know

We all face challenges in life. What has been a challenge for you? What keeps you from giving up? Write what you think on the lines below.

_____

_____

_____

_____

AGAINST ALL ODDS

Where there's a will, there's a way. This saying sums up baseball player Jim Abbott's life. On September 19, 1967, in Flint, Michigan, Abbott was born without fingers on his right hand. His parents, however, treated him as they would treat any other child. Abbott grew up thinking he could do anything. Despite having no fingers on his hand, his hard work has made him fulfill his lifelong dream of pitching in the major leagues.

At the age of five, Abbott began to notice other children playing ball. The sight of children throwing and catching the ball made him want to play, too. When he asked his father to teach him to catch, he was handed a baseball mitt. As they threw the ball to each other, his father told Jim to do whatever felt natural. Abbott developed his own way to throw and catch the ball. When he pitches, Abbott throws the ball with his left hand. He rests the palm of his glove on his right. After each pitch he quickly switches the glove to his left hand so he can catch.

As a child Abbott practiced throwing and catching for many hours every day. Pretending he was pitcher in a baseball game, he would send the ball exactly where he wanted it. As he practiced, Abbott would throw the ball against a brick wall. He would move closer and closer to the wall. That way he would have less time to catch the ball as it bounced back. Abbott did this to improve his speed. All of his hard work has paid off. As a thin boy of 11 he joined a little league team. In his very first game, he pitched a no-hitter.

Little league was just the beginning for Abbott. When he entered high school he became a star athlete. He was the starting quarterback for his high school football team. He helped the team get to the Michigan state finals. But his heart still belonged to baseball. After all, baseball was the national pastime. Also, it was a game that Abbott was very good at. While still in high school, he showed great promise as a pitcher. In fact, he showed so much promise that the Toronto Blue Jays drafted him. However, Abbott decided to go to college before becoming a pro. After he graduated from high school, Abbott accepted a baseball scholarship to the University of Michigan, where he continued to be a great player. At Michigan, he had a career record of 26 wins and 8 losses.

In addition to school teams, Abbott played ball as a member of Team USA. In 1987, he and the team went to Cuba. Abbott became the first American pitcher in 25 years to beat a Cuban team on their own field. Team USA won a silver medal in the Pan-American Games. Abbott won the U.S. Baseball Federation's Golden Spikes award as the best new player in the country. He wasn't through yet. In 1988, he played on the U.S. Olympic baseball team. Abbott pitched a 5–3 victory over the Japanese. This helped the U.S. win its first gold medal in baseball.

Jim Abbott believes that success is due to hard work and a little bit of luck. Do you agree? Why or why not? Write what you think on the lines below. Then keep reading to find out more about him.

_____

_____

_____

_____

Abbott is one of a group of great pitchers. His fastball **clocks in** at over 90 miles an hour. Abbott is unlike most professional players, because he never played in the minor leagues. Right after college Abbott went straight into the majors. In the first round of the 1988 draft, he was chosen by the California Angels to pitch for their team. He pitched for the Angels for four years. But it was as a pitcher for the New York Yankees that Abbott had the best game of his career. On September 4, 1993, he pitched a no-hitter against the Cleveland Indians.

Sportswriters described the day as a muggy afternoon. A stream of hot air rolled over the stadium. Abbott amazed the crowd and Cleveland's players with his **sinking** fastballs. After striking out players 23 times, Abbott had pitched a no-hitter.

In his usual way, Abbott said, "Every no-hitter takes a bit of luck."

It is surprising to learn that some people told Abbott he would not go far in sports. Abbott says he never agreed with the people who tried to hold him back. He knew that with enough hard work he could reach his dreams. He thinks others should work for their dreams every day. Even if you are tired and **feeling low,** Abbott says, don't give up. He believes you should stick it out to the end. Believe in yourself even when you have doubts and worries.

Perhaps this is why today Abbott speaks up for other disabled athletes. In a recent newspaper article, he stated his position about the Professional Golf Association's appeal to the Supreme Court. They wanted to bar disabled golfers from using carts during events. Abbott said that he respects the rules of sports, but he thinks sports should include everyone. He doesn't think that excluding athletes with disabilities helps any game. Abbott said that Major League Baseball never changed any rules for him. However, he feels that rules should help players with disabilities. He added that such rules should not change the nature of the game.

How do you think someone like Abbott inspires all people? Write what you think on the lines below.

_____

_____

_____

_____

For Abbott, his work as an athlete has given greater rewards than mere dollars. He feels rich because he has been able to reach his dream. He explains, "I was born without any fingers on my right hand. Doesn't seem like much, but it brings some extra challenges. Sports were my way of feeling I was just like everyone else."

Abbott is a great athlete. He doesn't consider himself disabled. He doesn't think his hand is as big an issue as some people make it out to be. As a result, Abbott doesn't really enjoy the attention he gets. However, he doesn't try to run away from it, either. He accepts it because he knows his successes mean a lot to many people. He gets hundreds of letters a week from people telling him how he has inspired them to work hard to reach a goal. He knows how much his experience can mean to a disabled child. If he can serve as a role model to help people to follow their dreams, he believes it is worth the fuss. Abbott likes to tell people, "I believe you can do anything you want if you put your mind to it."

You Be the Judge

◆ 1. After high school, Jim Abbott could have gone straight into professional baseball, but he decided to go to college first. Do you think he made a good decision? Why or why not? Write what you think on the lines below.

_____

_____

_____

Think About the Story

Use Story Words

◆ **Directions:** Look at your list of story words on page 51. Write a story word on each line.

2. Abbott was born _____.

3. Abbott was a star _____ in high school.

4. Abbott played both football and _____ in school.

5. Abbott worked hard to _____ his pitching.

6. Abbott played ball for the major _____.

7. Abbott has _____ many people.

When Did It Happen?

◆ 8. Write a number from 1 to 5 in front of each event to show when it happened.

_____ Abbott pitched a no-hitter against the Cleveland Indians.

_____ Abbott pitched a no-hitter in his first little league game.

_____ Abbott was born with no fingers on his right hand.

_____ Abbott played on the U.S. Olympic baseball team.

_____ Abbott's father taught him to play catch.

Write Sentences About the Story

◆ **Directions:** Use words from the story to answer these questions.

9. How did Abbott improve his speed while throwing his ball against a brick wall?

_____

_____

10. What was unusual about Abbott's visit to Cuba with the United States team in 1987?

_____

_____

_____

11. How does Abbott know that his successes mean a lot to many people?

_____

_____

_____

12. How does Abbott feel about changing sports rules for players with disabilities?

_____

_____

_____

Words and Meanings

Directions: Think about how the **bold** words are used in the story. Then circle the words that show the meaning of each word or phrase.

13. When Abbott says even if you're **feeling low** don't give up, he means that _____.
    a. you're short
    b. you're mean
    c. your mood is sad

14. Abbott's fastballs **clock in** at over 90 miles an hour. This means they _____.
    a. punch a time clock
    b. are recorded at speeds greater than 90 miles an hour
    c. hit a clock

15. A **sinking** fastball is a _____.
    a. ball that is accidentally thrown into water
    b. slow fastball that does not reach the batter
    c. ball that dips in its path toward the batter

Chapter 1 Summary of Skills and Strategies

Let's look back at what you learned in Chapter 1.

Letters and Sounds

◆ You learned about. . .

- long vowel sounds **a, e, i, o,** and **u.**
- irregular spellings for long vowels; **e** spelled **ey, a** spelled **ey** and **eigh,** and **o** spelled **ough.**
- silent consonants **t, h, n, c, d, w, g, k, b, l,** and **p.**
- **hard** and **soft c** sounds.

Stories and Skills

◆ You learned about. . .

- a poet who taught himself to read while in prison.
- a girl who discovers the importance of time spent with her grandfather.
- a television talk-show host who overcame a childhood of poverty to become a very successful woman.
- how sometimes the biggest role models are the people closest to us.
- a baseball player who refused to allow a physical disability to keep him from reaching his dream.

◆ You learned. . .

- how to read a play.
- how looking ahead and using what you know can help you understand stories.

Words and Meanings

◆ You learned. . .

- to add **ed** to verbs to make them tell about the past.
- to add **ing** to verbs to tell about the present.
- to double a final consonant before adding **ed.**
- to change a final **y** to **i** before adding **ed.**
- to form plurals by adding **s** or **es.**
- to use (') and **'s** to form possessives of regular and irregular nouns.
- the suffixes **er, or, ar,** and **ist.**
- the prefixes **un, re, pre, dis, de, non, im,** and **in.**

This chapter review will give you a chance to show what you have learned.

Part A

Summing It Up: Letters and Sounds

▲
▲ ▶ The letters **a, e, i, o,** and **u** sometimes have a long vowel sound.

◆ **Directions:** Write the word on the line. Circle the letters that make the long vowel sound.

1. tame _____
2. comb _____
3. she _____
4. wife _____
5. boat _____

6. cute _____
7. gave _____
8. dime _____
9. me _____
10. grate _____

▲
▲ ▶ Long vowel sounds are sometimes made with **irregular** combinations of letters, such as **eigh, ough, ey,** and **ay.**

◆ **Directions:** Write the word on the line. Circle the letters that make the long vowel sound.

11. sleigh _____
12. key _____
13. though _____

14. tray _____
15. grey _____

▲
▲ ▶ The consonants **b, c, d, g, h, k, l, n, p, t,** and **w** are sometimes silent.

◆ **Directions:** Circle the silent consonants in these words.

16. night
17. ghost
18. raspberry
19. half
20. write

21. fasten
22. wrong
23. knowledge
24. scenery
25. receipt

26. hasten
27. knife
28. calf
29. column
30. debt

> ▲ ▶ Many words have a **VC/CCV** pattern.

◆ **Directions:** Write each word on the line. Divide the words into syllables.

31. humble _____
32. middle _____
33. steamship _____
34. jiggle _____
35. hundred _____

36. tremble _____
37. rabble _____
38. hamster _____
39. unknown _____
40. purple _____

◆ **Directions:** Write the letters on the lines. See how many words you can make.

| h | m | p | r | tw |

41. _____ amble
42. _____ imple
43. _____ iddle
44. _____ iddle
45. _____ iddle

46. _____ aggle
47. _____ uddle
48. _____ uddle
49. _____ uddle

> ▲ ▲ ▶ The letter **c** can make a **hard sound,** as in the word **can.** It can also make a **soft sound,** as in the word **city.**

◆ **Directions:** Read the words out loud. Write a **k** or an **s** after the word to tell what sound it begins with.

50. celery _____
51. clear _____
52. close _____
53. circle _____
54. cap _____

55. citrus _____
56. civil _____
57. clam _____
58. claim _____
59. cut _____

◆ **Directions:** A **hard** or **soft c** can also occur at or near the end of a word. Write a **k** or an **s** on the line to tell which sound appears at the end of these words.

60. mice _____
61. trick _____

62. choice _____
63. voice _____

64. stick _____

Part B

Summing It Up: More Word Work

> ▸ To make a word tell that something happened in the past, add **ed.**
>
> ▸ For words that end in silent **e,** just add **d.**
>
> ▸ For words that end in a **consonant, double the final letter** and add **ed.**
>
> ▸ For words that end in **y, change y to an i** and add **ed.**

Directions: Add **ed** to the words below.

1. marry _____
2. chip _____
3. save _____
4. brave _____
5. plot _____

6. carry _____
7. bury _____
8. spot _____
9. kid _____
10. believe _____

> ▸ For most **nouns,** add **s** to make it **plural.**
>
> ▸ For many **nouns** that end in **o,** add **es** to make it **plural.**

Directions: Add **s** or **es** to the words below to make them plural.

11. car _____
12. hero _____

13. tomato _____
14. tree _____

> ▸ To show singular possession, add an apostrophe (') and an **s** to the word.
>
> ▸ To show possession for plural words ending in **s,** add only an apostrophe (').
>
> ▸ Nouns that change their form when they become plural are called **irregular plurals.**
>
> ▸ To show possession for irregular plurals that end in **s,** add an apostrophe (').
>
> ▸ For irregular plurals that do not end in **s,** add an apostrophe (') and an **s.**

Directions: Read the word. Make it possessive. Then write the new word on the line in the sentence.

15. doctors   The _____ coats were white.

16. grocer   The _____ aprons were clean.

17. workmen   The _____ lunches were ready.

18. wolves   The _____ tracks were fresh.

19. shoes   The _____ fit were too tight.

> ▶ The suffixes **er, or, ar,** and **ist** mean **one who does,** or **one who is.** They are found at the end of many words.

Directions: Add **er, or, ar,** or **ist** to the word parts below.

20. act _____   23. teach _____

21. dent _____   24. play _____

22. begg _____

> ▶ The **prefixes pre, in, im, dis, de, non, re,** and **un** are found at the beginning of many words.

Directions: Circle the correct word for each prefix. Write the new word on the line.

25. im (port/proud)   _____

26. pre (take/fix)   _____

27. in (deed/done)   _____

28. non (verbal/way)   _____

29. dis (here/belief)   _____

30. de (pend/plus)   _____

31. pre (tend/like)   _____

32. im (done/polite)   _____

33. re (peat/begin)   _____

34. un (done/go)   _____

Part C

Story Words

◆ **Directions:** On the lines below, write the word from the list that matches each clue.

celebrated	convict	awkward	courage
survival	revenge	savior	

1. criminal _____

2. to get even _____

3. famous _____

4. helper _____

5. taking care of life's basic needs _____

6. uncomfortable, not graceful _____

7. bravery _____

◆ **Directions:** On the lines below, write a word from the list to finish each sentence.

experienced	television	troop
elements	saluting	princess

8. The soldiers were all _____ their general.

9. Hydrogen and oxygen are the _____ that make up water.

10. The scout _____ went camping.

11. She was given the role of the _____.

12. He _____ many changes over the summer.

13. He prefers _____ talk shows to those on the radio.

◆ **Directions:** Read each word. On the lines below write a number to tell how many syllables it has.

14. improve _____   16. television _____

15. memories _____   17. celebrated _____

Directions: On the lines below, write the word from the list that matches each clue.

| humble | audience | tomorrow | ballet | rural |
| scholarship | library | admire | emulate | |

18. a place to borrow a book _____

19. a dance _____

20. the people who watch a performance _____

21. to be modest _____

22. an award of money to go to school _____

23. not in the city _____

24. not yesterday or today _____

25. to like someone or something _____

26. to be like someone else _____

Directions: On the lines below, write a word from the list to finish each sentence.

| assignment | disabled | baseball | inspired |
| league | athlete | memories | |

27. The homework _____ was interesting.

28. She was chosen for the high school _____ team.

29. He was _____ by poetry.

30. She was president of the bowling _____.

31. A _____ person is often talented in many other ways.

32. He was a good _____.

33. Her _____ of school were happy ones.

Directions: On the lines below, write a word from the list that matches each clue.

| orphanage | poverty | impression | duality | recipient |

34. the state of being poor _____

35. all things have more than one side _____

36. one who receives _____

37. home for children without parents _____

38. poetry uses senses to make this _____

Part D

Think About the Stories

Fiction or Nonfiction?

◆ **Directions:** Write **fiction** next to the stories that were made up by the writer. Write **nonfiction** next to the stories that tell about real life.

1. "It's Never Too Late" _____

2. "Birthday Party" _____

3. "Oprah Winfrey" _____

4. "Role Models" _____

5. "Against All Odds" _____

Who Did What?

◆ **Directions:** Answer each question with the name of a person from the stories in Chapter 1.

Jimmy Santiago Baca **Oprah Winfrey** **Carol**
Shaquana **Jim Abbott** **Antonio**

6. Who pitched a no-hitter? _____

7. Who admired her mother most of all people? _____

8. Who became a famous talk-show host? _____

9. Who wanted to go to the movies? _____

10. Who taught himself to read? _____

11. Who volunteered for Big Brothers? _____

Why Did It Happen?

◆ **Directions:** Draw a line from each cause in Column A to its effect in Column B.

Column A	Column B
12. Because Carol had to do some research,	◯ he told Chris he could not play ball.
13. Because little Jim Abbott wanted to learn to play ball,	◯ she told stories to the farm yard animals.
14. Because Oprah Winfrey loved to be the center of attention,	◯ she went to the library.
15. Because Jimmy Santiago Baca was angry with the prison guard,	◯ he stole a book.
16. Because Shaquana liked her friend Moesha,	◯ he asked his father to teach him to catch.
17. Because Antonio was volunteering as a Big Brother,	◯ she wanted to go to the movies with her.

CHAPTER 2

Letters and Sounds

◆ **Directions:** The letter **g** is a consonant. Read the words. Write them on the lines. Circle each letter **g**.

1. ago _____   4. gold _____

2. government _____   5. ginger _____

3. village _____

◆ **Directions:** The letter **g** has a soft and hard sound. The **g** sound in **gym** is a soft **g**. The **g** sound in **good** is a hard **g**. Circle the words below that begin or end with a soft **g**.

6. gem   8. edge   10. get   12. language

7. log   9. germ   11. judge   13. pig

◆ **Directions:** Circle the words below that begin or end with a hard **g**.

14. glue   16. fog   18. go   20. gave

15. good   17. fudge   19. huge   21. girl

> **TIP:** Words like **glue** and **good** have the vowel-vowel pattern.
> Another way to say vowel-vowel is V/V.

◆ **Directions:** Write the letters on the lines. See how many words you can make.

b	f	sl	h	tr	c	gr

22. _____ og   28. _____ udge

23. _____ og   29. _____ udge

24. _____ og   30. _____ udge

25. _____ og   31. _____ udge

26. _____ og   32. _____ udge

27. _____ og

Story Words

◆ **Directions:** Read each word to yourself. Then say the word out loud. Write the word on the line. Check the box after each step.

33. rhythm   Read ❑ Say ❑ Write ❑ _____

34. planets (plan│ets)   Read ❑ Say ❑ Write ❑ _____

35. astronomy   Read ❑ Say ❑ Write ❑ _____
       (as│tron│o│my)

36. telescope   Read ❑ Say ❑ Write ❑ _____
       (tel│e│scope)

37. observe (ob│serve)   Read ❑ Say ❑ Write ❑ _____

More Word Work

The ending **er** means "more." The ending **est** means "most." You can add **er** or **est** to many descriptive words.

Example: A baseball is bigger than a golf ball,
             but a basketball is the biggest of all three.

◆ **Directions:** Add **er** or **est** to the words below. Write the new word on the line.

38. tall   +   er   =   _____

39. kind   +   est   =   _____

40. fast   +   er   =   _____

41. loud   +   er   =   _____

42. rich   +   est   =   _____

> **TIP:** Use an adjective that ends in **er,** also called a **comparative** adjective, when you compare two things. When you compare more than two things, use an adjective that ends in **est,** which is called a **superlative.**

◆ **Directions:** Circle the correct word for the sentences below.

43. A car is (smaller / smallest) than a truck.

44. The winner of the marathon is the (faster / fastest) runner.

45. A bear is (bigger / biggest) than a dog.

46. A shout is (louder / loudest) than a whisper.

47. The Empire State Building was once the (taller / tallest) building in the world.

Use What You Know

José is starting the year at a new school. We all begin new things at different times in our lives. How does it feel to be in a new place where you don't know anyone? Write what you think on the lines below. Then read on to find out how José feels about being in a new school.

_____

_____

_____

FINDING NEW FRIENDS, PART 1

Ding! The bell was loud. In an instant, door after door opened and students flowed into the long hallway. José held his ground the best he could. He turned first this way, then that way, as students whirled past him. He remembered what his mother had said at breakfast that morning. "Today's an exciting day. Just think of all the new friends you're going to make."

José felt **invisible** as he watched the boys and girls, laughing and talking all around him. He wanted to feel excited but he was scared. He said to himself, "They all know where they're going. They already know each other. How will I ever make friends?"

Just then José felt a hand on his shoulder. He looked up into the smiling face of a tall man. "You must be José," the man said. "I'm Principal Wang, welcome to Franklin High School."

"Thank you, sir," said José.

Principal Wang turned to a small boy **hunched over** from the weight of a huge backpack. "This is Peter," said the principal. "He'll be your guide for your first week."

Peter pushed his glasses up on his nose and reached out to shake José's hand. "Hi," he said. "We have most of the same classes, so I'll show you around. I'll make sure you don't get lost or anything."

Ding! The bell rang again. "That's the first period bell. You boys had better get to class. And don't worry about anything, José. You'll soon get into the rhythm of things here." The principal smiled and walked away.

All week Peter showed José how to get around school. He introduced him to his friends. He told him important things like which teachers would allow you to do extra-credit work. He told him which books would be necessary to bring every day. He told him never to order the meatloaf in the cafeteria. Most important of all, he told him never to be late for Mr. Brown's science class.

"You see this?" Peter pulled a long metal tube out of his book bag. "Mr. Brown knows I'm interested in the planets and stars. I told him I'm planning to major in astronomy at college, so he loaned me this telescope. He's nice, but he's also strict. His class is one of the hardest in the school. If you get to his class even eight seconds after the late bell rings, he won't let you in. He sends you to the principal's office. Believe me, you don't want to end up there."

José liked Peter. He was a lot like José's friends at his old school. They were the kids who always did their homework. They were the kids whom all the teachers and parents liked. Yes, José liked his new friend, but sometimes he thought maybe Peter was a little dull. He wondered what it would be like to have a friend who was funnier. He wondered what it would be like to have a friend whom his parents and teachers might not like, someone like Fearless.

Everybody in school knew Fearless. The boy's real name was Stan, but the kids called him Fearless. They all thought he was the funniest kid in school. But the teachers didn't always laugh at his jokes. Fearless had a gag in Mr. Brown's class. Every day he would get to class the latest, just as the late bell rang. It drove Mr. Brown crazy the way the kids would laugh. Fearless would high-five his way to the back of the room.

One day in class, Fearless sat at the desk next to José's. José smiled at him, but Fearless just turned away and put his head down on the desk. José sat back to listen to the teacher. Soon he heard a strange sound. He looked over at Fearless. The noise was coming from the boy. Softly, at first, then louder and louder— "Snuchh, shhhhhh. Snuchh, shhhhh."

What do you think Fearless is doing? Circle your answer.
sneezing   taking notes   sleeping   listening to music
Then keep reading to find out what Fearless is doing.

Fearless was snoring! Every eye in the classroom turned to observe him. The teacher called out, "Stan! There is no sleeping in my class."

Fearless lifted his head from the desk. "I wasn't sleeping. I was just resting. I heard every word you said."

"Oh really," said Mr. Brown. "Then I'm sure you can tell us one part of the scientific process."

Fearless looked at Mr. Brown. Everyone waited for Fearless to speak. José whispered out of the side of his mouth, "Experimentation, experimentation."

"Uh, you know," said Fearless. "Experiments."

Mr. Brown looked surprised but said nothing.

The next day in the lunchroom Fearless called out to José and Peter. "Hey, come here. You're José, right?"

"Yeah," said José.

"That was pretty cool what you did in class yesterday, thanks."

"Oh yeah, well, I just wanted to help," said José.

Fearless nodded to some boys sitting with him. "This is Kenny, Rick, and Chucky."

"Hi," said José.

"Hey," said the boys.

"Hello," said Peter.

Fearless pointed to some empty chairs at the table and said, "Sit down."

José quickly pulled out a chair and sat down. He looked up at Peter. His friend didn't say anything. Then, slowly, Peter sat down, too.

José couldn't believe his luck. He thought Fearless was the coolest kid he had ever known. He was glad to be sitting with him and his friends. However, for some reason, José avoided looking at Peter.

Clang! Fearless dropped his fork on the table. He poked at a soggy fishcake on his plate. "This isn't food," he grumbled. "It's garbage."

The boys laughed loudly. "The meatloaf is even worse," said José. "Why don't they serve hot dogs or pizza?"

"That's a great idea," Fearless smiled. "Let's get pizza!"

"Boy, could I go for a slice," said Kenny.

Rick started to pound the table and Chucky joined in. "Pizza, pizza!" the two boys chanted.

The lunchroom **monitor** walked by, "Calm down boys."

Fearless quieted his friends. He leaned in and whispered, "Who wants to get pizza?"

José whispered back, "What do you mean? Now?"

Fearless nodded, "Let's go to the mall and get some real food."

"You can't leave school," said Peter.

"Why not?" Chucky grinned.

Peter ignored him and turned to José, "Mr. Brown is reviewing for tomorrow's science test. You better not miss class."

"We won't miss class," said Fearless. "We'll be back before the period starts."

"I suppose you think you can just walk in and out the front door without being stopped," said Peter.

"We'll use the back door. The one by the stairs next to Mr. Brown's class," said Fearless.

"That door is always locked," said Peter.

Fearless nodded, "That's why we need you to wait by it at the beginning of the period. When we knock, you open the door."

Peter turned to José, "Don't do this. Don't get in trouble your first week in school."

José looked at Peter. He looked at Fearless. "If I don't do this now," José thought to himself, "Fearless will never be my friend."

José pushed his food tray away. "I'm still hungry," he said.

Fearless smiled and slapped José on the back. "That's the way to do it," he said.

Peter shook his head sadly. "Okay, but if you're not back before the late bell rings, I'm going to class." ▶

You Be the Judge

◆ 1. José is cutting class to impress a new friend. Is it worth doing something you think is wrong to make a friend? What should he have said when Fearless asked him to go eat pizza? Write what you think on the lines below.

_____

_____

_____

Think About the Story

Use Story Words

◆ **Directions:** Look at your list of story words on page 69. Write a story word on each line.

2. The class turned to _____ Fearless snoring.

3. _____ is the study of outer space.

4. A _____ is used to see things from a distance.

5. Peter was interested in the _____ and stars.

6. Principal Wang told José he would get into the _____ of school.

When Did it Happen?

◆ 7. Write a number from 1 to 5 in front of each event to show when it happened.

_____ José helps Fearless in science class.

_____ José decides to cut class.

_____ Peter shows José around school.

_____ José goes to a new school.

_____ Fearless asks José to cut class.

Write Sentences About the Story

◆ **Directions:** Circle the word that best fits in each sentence. Then write the sentence on the line.

8. Ding! The bell was (louder / loud).

_____

9. José thought Peter was (dull / duller) than Fearless.

_____

10. Mr. Brown's class was one of the (harder / hardest) in school.

_____

11. Peter thought Mr. Brown was a (nice / nicer) teacher.

_____

Words and Meanings

◆ **Directions:** Think about how the **bold** words are used in the story. Then circle the words that show the meaning of each word or phrase.

12. José feels **invisible** because _____.
   a. no one talks to him at school
   b. he can't see himself in the mirror
   c. he can walk through walls

13. A small boy **hunched over** from the weight of a backpack was _____.
   a. guessing its contents
   b. bent over
   c. propelled across the room

14. The **monitor** in the lunchroom is _____.
   a. a computer display
   b. a large tropical lizard
   c. a student assistant

Look Ahead

◆ 15. Who do you think will prove to be a better friend? Should José listen to Peter or to Fearless? Write what you think on the lines below. Then read on to find out what happens.

_____

_____

_____

Letters and Sounds

◆ **Directions:** The letters **ough** and **augh** appear in many words. Read the words below. Write the word on the line. Then circle the letters **ough** or **augh**.

1. through _____   3. caught _____

2. fought _____   4. naughty _____

◆ **Directions:** The letters **ough** have different sounds in different words. These **ough** words all have the sound like the letter **o** in the word **lost**. Read these words. Write them on the lines.

5. thought _____   7. sought _____

6. fought _____

◆ **Directions:** These **ough** words all have the sound like the letter **ou** in the word **out**. Read these words. Write them on the lines.

8. bough _____   10. sough _____

9. plough _____

◆ **Directions:** These **ough** words all sound like the letter **u** in the word **cut**. Read these words. Write them on the lines.

11. enough _____   12. rough _____

◆ **Directions:** Write the letters on the lines. See how many words you can make.

b	f	s	th	thr	tr	pl	en	c	l	t

13. _____ augh   20. _____ ough

14. _____ ought   21. _____ ough

15. _____ ought   22. _____ ough

16. _____ ought   23. _____ ough

17. _____ ought   24. _____ ough

18. _____ aught   25. _____ ough

19. _____ aught   26. _____ ough

◆ **Directions:** These words have three syllables. Write each word on the line. Draw a line between each syllable.

27. general _____   29. remember _____

28. connection _____   30. janitor _____

Story Words

◆ **Directions:** Read each word to yourself. Then say the word out loud. Write the word on the line. Check the box after each step.

Word Bank

Write each of these story words in the Word Bank at the back of this book.

31. army (ar│my)   Read ❑ Say ❑ Write ❑ _____

32. property
      (prop│er│ty)   Read ❑ Say ❑ Write ❑ _____

33. particular
      (par│tic│u│lar)   Read ❑ Say ❑ Write ❑ _____

34. conference
      (con│fer│ence)   Read ❑ Say ❑ Write ❑ _____

35. gestured (ges│tured) Read ❑ Say ❑ Write ❑ _____

36. disappointed
      (dis│ap│point│ed)   Read ❑ Say ❑ Write ❑ _____

More Word Work

◆ **Directions:** You can add the letters **ly** to many words. Add **ly** to make a word tell how something was done. Add **ly** to each word.

Example: quick   quick + ly = quickly

37. soft   _____   40. bad   _____

38. slow   _____   41. loud   _____

39. glad   _____

> **TIP:**   A suffix is an ending added to a word. The letters **ly** form a suffix. The endings **ful, less, ness, ment**, and **y** are also suffixes.

◆ **Directions:** Add the suffixes to the words below. Write the word on the line.

Example: harm + less = harmless

42. wish + ful =   _____

43. care + less =   _____

44. retire + ment =   _____

45. tall + ness =   _____

46. spook + y =   _____

Use What You Know

To impress his new friend, José has broken school rules. Will he be sorry? Write what you think on the lines below. Then read on to find out what happens.

_____

_____

_____

_____

FINDING NEW FRIENDS, PART 2

The boys gathered at the door by the stairwell near Mr. Brown's class. Fearless took a hat out of his pocket and fit it snugly on his head. He spoke as if he were a general in the army. "Listen up boys," he said. "Our **mission** is to get through that door, across the parking lot, and off school property."

Chucky began to chant in a low voice, "Pizza, pizza, pizza!"

Chucky became quiet when Fearless glared at him. "We better watch out for Principal Wang. He keeps an eye on the parking lot at this time of day."

José swallowed hard. Peter touched his arm and said, "Are you sure you want to do this?"

José pretended to feel brave. He shrugged free of Peter's hand. "I said so, didn't I?"

"Yeah, Peter," said Fearless. "Just remember to be here to open the door at the beginning of next period."

"I'll be here," frowned Peter.

"Okay, everybody follow me." Fearless opened the door and poked his head outside. He turned to the boys. "We're moving out. Let's go!"

One by one the boys slipped out the door. Fearless and Rick were in front of José. Chucky and Kenny were behind him. José felt as if he were caught in a strong current. His only choice was to swim along with the others. They kept low, moving from car to car. Suddenly Fearless called out, "Get down!"

All five boys dropped to their knees. José heard a loud banging noise. He raised his head and peeked over the hood of the car. The school janitor was emptying trash into a bin. The janitor finished and went back inside the school. José breathed a sigh of relief. Fearless called out, "Let's move."

Again the boys moved from car to car. With shouts of glee they turned the corner away from school. Once more Chucky began a chant of "Pizza, pizza, pizza!" This time all the boys joined in.

The mall was only a couple of minutes from school. Soon the boys found themselves in front of the pizza shop. They entered and marched straight to the counter. The man behind the counter looked at the clock on the wall. He said, "Aren't you boys supposed to be in school?"

"No," Fearless lied. "It's a half day today."

"Yeah," Kenny added. "Teachers and parents conference."

"In that case, what can I do for you?"

"We want pizza," said Rick.

"Then you boys are in luck, because that's what I sell."

The boys paid for their food and sat down in a booth to eat. The pizza was hot and cheesy. The tomato sauce was spicy. It was very good pizza. José hardly tasted it.

Fearless poked him, "Hey, this was a great idea."

"It's good pizza," said José.

"It's the best," said Fearless. "We're lucky Peter doesn't have the guts to do anything but wait at the door for us."

José felt that he should defend Peter, but he didn't know what to say. He took a bite of pizza instead.

Have you ever wanted to defend a friend? What should José have said to Fearless? Write what you think on the lines below. Then keep reading to find out what takes place.

_____

_____

Just then Chucky wadded up a napkin and threw it at Rick who yelled, "Hey! What are you doing?"

"Sorry," said Chucky, "I was trying to hit Kenny."

"Then you'll pay!" said Kenny. He threw a napkin at Chucky. Soon all the boys were laughing and throwing napkins. All of the boys fought except José. He sat still, not knowing what to do.

The man behind the counter called out, "Boys, you can't do that in here!"

The boys jumped up and ran out of the store laughing. José picked up the napkins his friends had thrown and put them in the garbage can. He looked at the man and said, "Sorry mister."

When the boys got back to school they could see Peter holding open the door. They raced toward him. José tripped, and his feet flew out from under him. He landed on the ground. Looking up, he saw sneakers and blue jeans racing by him. José heard the door slam shut. He leaped up and ran toward the door. He pulled on it. It was locked and wouldn't open. He knocked on the door. He pounded on the door.

Then a hand touched his shoulder. José was fearful as he turned around. "I think you better come with me," said Principal Wang.

José sat in the waiting room outside Principal Wang's office. The door to the office was closed, but José could hear voices coming from inside. It sounded like Principal Wang and a student were talking. José wondered if Fearless or one of the other boys had been caught. He wondered what punishment he would get.

The door opened and Principal Wang gestured for José to come in. He got up and slowly walked into the office. José looked at the other student. "Peter!"

José sat down. Principal Wang looked sternly at the two boys. "José, I'm hoping you can help me understand something. I found you outside banging on the back door to the school. Mr. Brown also found Peter inside hanging around the back door. It seems to me there must be a connection between these two events. However, Peter has chosen not to say anything. Can you tell me what was going on, José?"

"Well," mumbled José.

"Speak up. I can't hear you."

"Sorry, sir. I guess I went to get some pizza at the mall, sir."

"Are you aware that it is against school rules to leave the grounds?"

"Yes sir," said José. "But Peter had nothing to do with it. I just wanted some pizza so I left."

Principal Wang looked at Peter. He looked at José. "I'm very disappointed in you José. Your first week at Franklin High School and you break a very important rule. I'm afraid I'm going to have to call your parents."

Peter sat up in his chair. "Please don't do that! I'm José's guide. I'm supposed to make sure his first week is a good one. It's my fault, sir."

Principal Wang turned to José and asked, "Do you think that's true?"

"No," said José. "Peter tried to stop me, but I wouldn't listen."

Principal Wang was quiet for a long time. Then he said, "I am very **particular** about students following the rules. I know Peter. He is always willing to do the right thing. Since you are new, José, I am willing to give you the benefit of the doubt. Just this one time, I will not call your parents. I will not call either of your parents. But you must both stay after school today. Will you accept these terms?" Both boys nodded.

Out in the hall the two boys looked at each other. José said, "What happened to Fearless and the others?"

"They heard Mr. Brown coming and ran up the stairs. He took me away before I could let you back in. So, did you have fun?"

"Not really," said José. "They were acting like fools when we got the pizza. I think I prefer a friend like you that I can count on."

"Yeah, me too," said Peter.

The two boys smiled and walked back to class.

—————————————◆—————————————

You Be the Judge

1. At first, José thought that Fearless was exciting and that Peter was dull. Who do you think was really the better friend, Peter or Fearless? Write what you think on the lines below.

_____

_____

Think About the Story

Use Story Words

Directions: Look at your list of story words on page 77. Write a story word on each line.

2. A _____ is a meeting.

3. Students were not allowed to leave school _____.

4. Principal Wang _____ for José to come in.

5. Fearless spoke to the boys like an _____ general.

6. The principal was very _____ about students following rules.

7. Principal Wang was _____ in José.

When Did It Happen?

8. Write a number from 1 to 5 in front of each event to show when it happened.

_____ José trips and falls.

_____ José, Fearless, and some boys cut class.

_____ José and Peter walk back to class.

_____ The boys throw napkins in the pizza parlor.

_____ The principal catches José.

Write Sentences About the Story

Directions: Use words from the story to answer these questions.

9. What does José do when Peter asks him if he really wants to sneak out for pizza?

_____

_____

10. How do the boys respond when the counter man at the pizza shop says, "Aren't you boys supposed to be in school?"

_____

_____

11. When Principal Wang asks him to explain why he was outside banging on the back door to the school, what does José say?

_____

_____

Words and Meanings

Directions: Think about how the **bold** words are used in the story. Then circle the words that show the meaning of each word or phrase.

12. Fearless said, "Our **mission** is to get through that door." Here mission means a _____.
    a. church
    b. goal or aim
    c. business

13. Principal Wang said, "I am very **particular** about students following the rules." Here particular means _____.
    a. concerned over details
    b. not interested
    c. happy

Why Did It Happen?

Directions: Draw a line from each story event to the reason it happened.

Event	Reason
14. The pizza store owner kicked out the boys from his shop.	○ Mr. Brown took him away from the door.
15. Peter did not open the door for José.	○ The boys were throwing napkins.
16. José was taken to the principal's office.	○ He was caught cutting class.

Letters and Sounds

◆ **Directions:** These words have a long **e** vowel sound. They are spelled with an **ie** and sound like the letters **ee** in the word **bleed.** Write the word on the line. Circle the vowels that make the **e** sound in each word.

1. believe _____   3. brief _____

2. piece _____   4. relief _____

◆ **Directions:** These words have the long **a** vowel sound. They are spelled with **ei** as in the word **neighbor.** Write the word on the line. Circle the vowels that make the long **a** in each word.

5. freight _____   7. eight _____

6. vein _____   8. reign _____

> **TIP:** Here is a rhyme to help you remember an **ei/ie** spelling rule. Use **i** before **e** when sounded as **ee**, except after **c**, or when sounded like **a**, as in **neighbor** and **weigh.**

◆ **Directions:** As the rhyme reminds us, we use **ei** after the letter **c.** The word **conceit** is an example. Write the word on the line. Circle the vowels **ei** in each word.

9. receive _____   11. perceive _____

10. deceit _____   12. ceiling _____

◆ **Directions:** The **ei** after **c** rule does not always work. We use **i** before **e** when **c** has a **sh** sound. The word **glacier** is an example. Write the word on the line. Circle the **ie** in each word.

13. ancient _____   15. conscience _____

14. species _____

◆ **Directions:** Below are some words that are missing the letters **ei** or **ie.** Write the correct letters on the line to complete the words.

16. f_____ld   19. w_____ght   22. sl_____gh

17. rec_____pt   20. dec_____ve   23. w_____gh

18. sh_____ld   21. th_____f   24. p_____rce

Story Words

Word Bank

Write each of these story words in the Word Bank at the back of this book.

◆ **Directions:** Read each word to yourself. Then say the word out loud. Write the word on the line. Check the box after each step.

25. partner (part│ner)   Read ❑ Say ❑ Write ❑ _____

26. permanent
    (per│ma│nent)   Read ❑ Say ❑ Write ❑ _____

27. pedestrian
    (pe│des│tri│an)   Read ❑ Say ❑ Write ❑ _____

28. enduring
    (en│dur│ing)   Read ❑ Say ❑ Write ❑ _____

More Word Work

◆ **Directions:** Two words can be put together to make a new word called a **compound word.** The compound word usually has a new and different meaning from the words that make it. Use the list to find a match for each word below. Write the matching word on the line. Then write the new compound word.

Example: back + yard = backyard

car   book   seed   cloth   pin

29. hand + _____ = _____

30. table + _____ = _____

31. bird + _____ = _____

32. box + _____ = _____

33. hair + _____ = _____

◆ **Directions:** Some compound words are joined with a hyphen (-) because the first word modifies the second. Some are not joined at all. Use the list to find a match for each word below. Write the matching word on the line. Then write the new compound word.

Example: saddle + blanket = saddle blanket

eye   bus   -eater   wool

34. school + _____ = _____

35. fire + _____ = _____

36. eagle + _____ = _____

37. steel + _____ = _____

Use What You Know

At times we all need to learn new skills. What is the most difficult thing you ever learned? How did you feel when you learned it? Write about it on the lines below.

_____

_____

_____

SECOND SIGHT

Dogs are often called man's best friend. For those who are blind, a dog is more than friendly company. A dog is a pair of **sharp** eyes. A trained dog guide gives blind people the freedom to move through the world safely and freely. A dog guide is also a best friend.

Becoming a working team of a dog and a person is not easy. There are no factories making thousands of dog guides a day. There are, however, schools all over the country that train both blind people and the dogs they depend upon. The process of education is long for both the dog and its human partner.

A dog begins schooling as a puppy. Around the age of eight weeks, the puppy is placed with a foster family. There it receives training and gets used to being around people. When the dog is about a year old, it goes off to school for a series of tests. These tests help the school decide whether the dog is likely to make a good guide. Dogs that fail the tests are placed in permanent homes. Those that pass the tests go into a training program.

For the next four-to-six months, the dog learns everything it needs to become a dog guide. The dog learns to stay focused. It learns to ignore food, smells, and other animals. It learns to remain undistracted by such noises as shouting or music from a passing car radio. It learns to follow commands like "right," "left," or "forward." The dog learns to stop before every curb and stairway and to avoid moving objects. In short, good dog guides learn to keep their owners safe while they go about the everyday actions of life. A dog that has completed training will be assigned a master.

Before the dog guide and its new master can be united, the owner also has to undergo some training. Not every blind person is able to handle a dog. Just as the school tries to decide which dogs will make a good guide, they must also decide which people will be able to work well with a dog.

To be accepted as a student, each person must first undergo a medical exam. The school must be sure a person is in good shape. The person must also have a good sense of balance and direction. But most important, the school wants to find out if the person is the right kind of person to own a dog. To find this out, the school asks many questions: Do you enjoy a dog following you around your home? Do you enjoy a dog **tongue washing** your face? Have you ever owned a dog before? The school asks these and many other questions to learn if the person will be a good dog owner and student.

Once accepted, the student is still not quite ready to meet the new dog. First the student must attend classes to learn how to care for a dog. The student learns to bathe and brush a dog's hair, to clean a dog's ears, and brush its teeth. It is important to know what to feed a dog and what to do if the animal becomes sick.

Then comes instruction for putting a harness on the dog. The harness is a series of straps attached to a handle. The owner holds onto the harness while walking with the dog. The harness is a sign that the dog is on the job. The dog will know not to be distracted from guiding its partner. This is also the reason why you should never pet or distract a dog guide in harness.

After all these basics are learned, the moment that both dog and owner have been waiting for arrives. They meet each other.

What do you think the dog and owner must learn after they meet? Write what you think on the lines below. Then keep reading to find out how the new partners become a real team.

_____

_____

_____

Once dog and master are **matched,** the real work begins. For the next month, the two spend every hour of the day together. They work hard to become a team. At first they practice walking together on the school grounds. They walk the courses set up by their teachers. Then they take their first steps off school property. They take a walk around the block first. Soon they move about all the streets near the school. They walk in streets filled with mailboxes and newsstands, pedestrians, bicycles, and cars. They face all the things that sighted people take for granted.

For some, the hardest part of the training is learning to follow the dog. In his book _Walking with Smokie, Walking with Blindness,_ Rod Michalko describes his first experiences learning to follow his dog guide, Smokie. They had trouble on their first trip outside the school building. Rod was told to go to a field behind the school. The route to the field was familiar to him. Rod had been using it since his first days at the school. With Smokie's harness in his hand, Rod left the school. He turned left toward the field. Suddenly, Smokie began moving right. Rod knew that the sidewalk was to the left. He guided Smokie back toward the field. Rod's trainer told him to command Smokie to stay. He asked Rod if the word "guide" meant anything to him. The trainer then explained that Smokie was guiding Rod around a post that had been placed in the middle of the sidewalk.

But this experience was still not enough to teach Rod to follow his dog. Later that week he got into more serious trouble. Rod and Smokie were walking down the street at their usual fast pace. Then Smokie began to veer left. Thinking the dog was making a mistake, Rod did not follow. Just then he bumped into a parking meter. Rod felt the full force of the post in the middle of his chest. It was very painful. **From then on,** Rod always followed Smokie!

When their training is completed, the new dog guide team must get settled at home. Even though their schooling has ended, their learning continues. As long as the two are a team they will continue to learn about each other. They will learn each other's needs, likes, and dislikes. They will learn about the world around them. Rod says that when he and Smokie walk down the street, he forgets his blindness. He focuses on where he is going and the world around him. He also says that Smokie makes him experience his blindness in new ways. His dog helps him to think about what is truly important in life. He says, "Smokie is my guide, my partner, and my friend. My gratitude to Smokie is as eternal as my love for him."

For some, the only bond closer than the one they share with their dog guide is with their husband, wife, or child. They are partners with their dog guide. They know that without the help of their dog, their life would not be as fulfilling. Their partnership is a working one, but it is also an enduring friendship.

You Be The Judge

◈ 1. Dog-guide schools want to make sure their students are the right kind of person to own a dog guide. What kind of person do you think is best suited to owning a dog? Write what you think on the lines below.

_____

_____

2. Rod Michalko said that his blindness helps him to realize what is important. What do you think he means? What do you think is important?

_____

_____

Think About the Story

Use Story Words

◈ **Directions:** Look at your list of story words on page 85. Write a story word on each line.

3. A dog guide is trained to be a _____ for a sightless person.

4. A _____ walked along the sidewalk and then crossed the street.

5. An _____ relationship is one that lasts a long time.

6. Dogs that fail the dog guide test are placed in _____ homes.

The Big Idea

◈ 7. Circle the sentence that tells what the whole story is about.
   a. Never pet a dog guide in harness.
   b. People and dogs train a long time to work well as a team.
   c. Dog guides begin their training when they are still puppies.

Write Sentences About the Story

◆ **Directions:** Use words from the story to answer these questions.

8. How can you tell when a dog guide is on the job?

_____

_____

9. What was the hardest part of dog-guide training for Rod?

_____

_____

10. What must a person do before entering dog-guide school?

_____

_____

Words and Meanings

◆ **Directions:** Think about how the **bold** words are used in the story. Then circle the words that show the meaning of each word or phrase.

11. A dog guide has **sharp** eyes. What does this mean?

   a. The dog's eyes are pointy.

   b. The dog's eyelids are narrow.

   c. The dog has very good vision.

12. Do you enjoy a dog **tongue washing** your face? What does this mean?

   a. Do you mind if a dog beats you in a race?

   b. Do you mind when a dog touches you with its tongue?

   c. Do you like it when a dog puts its paws on you?

13. After running into a parking meter, Rod learned **from then on** to follow his dog. This means that _____.

   a. from that time on Rod followed his dog

   b. Rod pointed his dog in the right direction

   c. he got stuck with a needle

14. Once the dog and his master are **matched,** the real work begins. This means they are _____.

   a. given matches to light a fire

   b. made to look exactly alike

   c. paired as a team

Letters and Sounds

> **TIP:** The sound of the **i** in the word **easily** is called the **schwa** sound. The vowels **a, e, i, o, u** can all make the **schwa** sound. The **schwa** sound is usually in the unstressed part of the word.

◆ **Directions:** Write the words on the lines. Then circle the letters that make the **schwa** sound.

1. recommend _____
2. divide _____
3. license _____

4. suppose _____
5. compass _____

> **TIP:** The letter patterns **al, el, le, er, or, ar, es, is, ed, id, en, on,** and **ion** can all stand for the **schwa** sound.

◆ **Directions:** Write the words on the lines. Then circle the letters that make the schwa sound.

6. table _____
7. technical _____
8. maple _____
9. material _____
10. humor _____
11. flower _____
12. added _____
13. candid _____
14. particular _____

15. counter _____
16. piston _____
17. companion _____
18. person _____
19. listen _____
20. question _____
21. collision _____
22. decision _____
23. fasten _____

◆ **Directions:** The suffixes **sion** and **tion** are found at the end of many words. Circle the suffix that correctly completes the words below. Write the new word on the line.

24. posi (sion / tion) _____
25. inva (sion / tion) _____
26. preci (sion / tion) _____
27. addi (sion / tion) _____
28. crea (sion / tion) _____
29. colli (sion / tion) _____
30. tradi (sion / tion) _____

Story Words

◆ **Directions:** Read each word to yourself. Then say the word out loud. Write the word on the line. Check the box after each step.

31. southern   Read ❑ Say ❑ Write ❑ _____
    (south|ern)

32. bonus (bo|nus)   Read ❑ Say ❑ Write ❑ _____

33. boredom   Read ❑ Say ❑ Write ❑ _____
    (bore|dom)

34. yellow (yel|low) Read ❑ Say ❑ Write ❑ _____

More Word Work

◆ **Directions:** You can make a **contraction** by joining two words together. **I'm** is a contraction of the words **I** and **am.** Match the contractions with the two words that make them. Write the words on the line.

35. we'll   _____   a. it is

36. can't   _____   b. could have

37. it's   _____   c. we would

38. we'd   _____   d. we will

39. could've _____   e. can not

> ▶ **TIP:** When two words are joined to make one new word, letters are left out to shorten them. An apostrophe (') marks the place where letters are left out.

Word Bank

Write each of these story words in the Word Bank at the back of this book.

Use What You Know

This is a story about students who help other people. At times we all help others. How have you helped people around you? Did you work alone or with others? Write your answers on the lines below.

_____

_____

_____

STUDENT VOLUNTEER

Every year, over half of all students in the United States volunteer their time and **services.** While some simply collect money once a year for a favorite charity, others work hours each week for a group. Volunteers tutor other students and work in hospitals and homeless shelters. They help at daycare centers and senior citizen homes. They answer the phones at crisis centers. Though their level of help varies, volunteers all help society. Some even charge full-speed ahead and create volunteer groups of their own. Student volunteers give freely and, in the process, they gain many rewards.

Our country has a long tradition of volunteer service to others. In colonial times it was common for people to help each other. People would care for sick neighbors or bring food and clothing to families in need. By the middle of the 1800s, people who had formerly worked on their own

began to form groups to help others. Volunteer groups such as the Red Cross, Boys Clubs, Goodwill Industries, and the American Cancer Society were all formed during this period. These groups and many others like them continue their good work to this day.

Student volunteers come from many backgrounds, both rich and poor. They live in the cities and rural areas of the southern and northern states. They can also be found from east to west. They're male and female students with excellent and average grades. They represent every ethnic group, race, and religion. Though different in every possible way, volunteers share the belief that they can bring about change.

Jessica, a student at the University of Missouri in Columbia, explains why she volunteers. "I've been taught about the importance of giving back to the community all my life. I've assisted in holiday **drives** at school, and at church for families in need. As a high school student, I began to realize that volunteering was not just an activity that benefited nameless people in faraway places, but rather something that helped real families, just like mine, to get by during hard times. This motivated me to increase my own volunteering, as well as to talk my peers into such activities."

Like Jessica, many students volunteer because of a strong desire to make changes in the world. When they see a problem, such as homelessness, they want to help. That was why Priya, a student volunteer living in Atlanta, got involved in Habitat for Humanity. Habitat is a group that fights homelessness by building houses. Volunteers do everything from nailing down shingles to painting walls. Priya said, "I loved building for Habitat. It was hard but very gratifying." Priya doesn't feel helpless in the face of life's challenges. As a volunteer for Habitat, she helped many people. Learning new skills was a bonus.

Some students find volunteer work may help to build a résumé. This can be useful when applying to colleges or for a job. Jack had volunteered his services at many nonprofit theaters in Oklahoma City where he lives. He is a talented actor. Volunteering to work at theaters was something he loved to do. Jack also found that his volunteer work helped him to get a job he wanted. His theater credentials was a deciding factor in landing a part-time job with a film company. It's important to know that many employers, including federal and state governments, accept volunteer experiences as work history.

Besides being a good way to build a résumé, Jack also thinks that volunteering is fun. He describes a good volunteer experience he had. "As president of my high school's chapter of the National Honor Society, I volunteered our club to ring the Salvation Army bell at a local mall over Christmas break. Not enough of our members signed up for **shifts.** A few of us had to split up about twenty hours of leftover time. I was not too eager to ring the Salvation Army bell in the cold in five-hour shifts for two days in a row, but it turned out to be a great experience. After a couple of hours, our boredom overcame our embarrassment, and we started singing Christmas carols. It was a lot of goofy fun, and people seemed to be much more generous once we started singing."

Would you like to be a volunteer? Explain why or why not on the lines below.

_____

_____

_____

_____

Before volunteering, ask yourself what you'd like to get from it. Do you have a certain concern, such as pollution or the environment? Are you interested in learning a new skill or gaining things to put on your résumé? Do you have an interest or hobby, such as music or art that you want to share with others? Are you simply interested in meeting new people and making new friends? Once you've answered these questions, you're ready to seek out volunteer groups.

A good place to start your search is at your school library. The librarian can **direct** you to listings of volunteer groups. Another resource is the National Volunteer Center. There are offices located in states all across the country. They are ready and able to direct you to groups in your region.

If you see an unmet need in your area, you can start your own group. Maybe you would like to create a weekly story hour for neighborhood children. Maybe you could bring live music to senior citizen centers. Perhaps you see a need to teach the public about proper ways to recycle.

Whatever your goal, you'll need to get organized. A great place to form your group is at school. A teacher who is willing to advise you can help your group become an official student group. Schools can often provide space for meetings. Sometimes, they can even provide funding.

Student volunteers have done wonderful things to help their areas. They have painted kitchen walls yellow for Habitat for Humanity. They have sung Christmas carols and played the triangle for the Salvation Army. Students have printed collections of stories for literacy groups. They have loaded trucks to deliver food to the hungry. They have done all this and much more. It seems like the only thing students are unwilling to do is not try to make the world a better place.

Whether you start your own group or join an existing one, you'll find that the rewards of volunteering are great. You will make new friends, learn new skills, and learn things to help you get a job. And, perhaps most important, you will enjoy the feeling of helping others.

You Be the Judge

◆ 1. There are many different reasons to volunteer. Do you think students should volunteer? Why or why not? Write what you think on the lines below.

_____

_____

_____

Think About the Story

Use Story Words

◆ **Directions:** Look at your list of story words on page 93. Write a story word on each line.

2. Volunteers paint walls _____.

3. Student volunteers come from the northern, eastern, western, and _____ parts of our country.

4. When people complain of _____ they are usually to blame.

5. The good feeling volunteers gain is a _____ for their hard work.

Who Did What?

◆ **Directions:** Match the person or group with the correct sentence.

6. Priya _____   a. got a job with a film company.

7. Goodwill Industries _____   b. built houses for Habitat for Humanity.

8. Jack _____   c. is a student at the University of Missouri.

9. Student volunteers _____   d. was founded in the middle of the 1800s.

10. Jessica _____   e. come from all over the country.

Write Sentences About the Story

◆ **Directions:** Use words from the story to answer the questions.

11. Do many students in the United States care about helping other people?

_____

_____

12. Why do students volunteer to help other people?

_____

_____

13. What questions must you ask yourself if you want to do volunteer work?

_____

_____

Words and Meanings

◆ **Directions:** Think about how the **bold** words are used in the story. Then circle the words that show the meaning of each word or phrase.

14. Volunteers believe in **services** to others. Here services means _____.
    a. the army
    b. giving help
    c. going to church

15. The librarian can **direct** you to books about volunteer groups. Here direct means _____.
    a. the librarian can help you put on a show
    b. the librarian will be right with you
    c. the librarian can show you books

16. Jessica has assisted in holiday **drives** at school. Here drives means _____.
    a. an effort to raise money
    b. a car pool
    c. a trip

17. Jack said, "Not enough of our members signed up for **shifts**." He means _____.
    a. moving around
    b. work periods
    c. dresses

Lesson 4   **99**

Letters and Sounds

> **TIP:** The **a** vowel sound in **ago** is called the **schwa** sound. The letters **a, e, i, o, u, io,** and **le** can all stand for the **schwa** sound.

◆ **Directions:** Write the words on the lines. Then circle the **schwa** sounds.

1. person _____

2. listen _____

3. tragedy _____

4. direction _____

5. position _____

6. castle _____

7. wrestle _____

8. fasten _____

9. companion _____

10. collision _____

11. comedy _____

12. question _____

13. thimble _____

14. decision _____

> **TIP:** A **schwa** sound is usually in the unstressed part of the word.

◆ **Directions:** Write each word where it belongs in the chart.

| sleepily | noisily | whistle | castle |

| enlighten | whiten | soften | nestle |

happily	frighten	thistle
15. _____	17. _____	20. _____
16. _____	18. _____	21. _____
	19. _____	22. _____

Story Words

◆ **Directions:** Read each word to yourself. Then say the word out loud. Write the word on the line. Check the box after each step.

23. column (col|umn)   Read ❏ Say ❏ Write ❏   _____

24. molecules
     (mol|e|cules)   Read ❏ Say ❏ Write ❏   _____

25. repeated
     (re|peat|ed)   Read ❏ Say ❏ Write ❏   _____

26. western (west|ern)   Read ❏ Say ❏ Write ❏   _____

27. Paris (Par|is)   Read ❏ Say ❏ Write ❏   _____

More Word Work

◆ **Directions:** The letters **able** put together two **schwa** sounds at the end of many words such as **teachable**. The suffix **able** means "likely to" or "able to." Read the words. Write them on the lines.

28. capable   _____

29. durable   _____

30. portable   _____

31. peaceable   _____

◆ **Directions:** The letters **ible** put together two **schwa** sounds at the end of many words such as **eligible**. Read the words. Write them on the lines.

32. horrible   _____

33. visible   _____

34. credible   _____

35. terrible   _____

Use What You Know

Sometimes children in families do not get along well. What kinds of conflicts do brothers and sisters sometimes have? Write what you think on the lines below.

_____

_____

_____

_____

BLOOD BROTHERS, PART 1

All right, I admit it shouldn't have happened. But it was John's fault just as much as it was mine. John was way out of line. He gets away with everything. It's been that way ever since we were little. No matter what he did, it was always, "Todd, don't treat your brother like that. He's younger than you." I tell you, it's just not fair.

John and I are the exact opposite of each other. I play every sport there is. And I'm good at them all. My name is almost always in the sports column of our school newspaper. I guess I just like to have fun. I need fun everyday like I need oxygen to breathe. John's idea of fun is looking at molecules under a microscope. One year he repeated science class in summer school. He did it just so he could use the school lab. He said he

had some projects that couldn't wait until the fall. Do you have any idea how embarrassing it is to have a brother who talks like that? The fact that he talks like that is just one of the reasons I like to call him "nerds." Notice I said "nerds" not "nerd." He is such a nerd I have to use the plural form of the word. Calling him a nerd isn't enough. John is definitely "nerds."

Anyway, I guess the fight started the night Karen told everyone that she was getting married. Karen's our sister. She was a senior in college then, but she was home for the weekend. So she and the whole family came to my basketball game, and it was great. We were playing our biggest rivals, and the score was close right up to the end. I had a great game. I was the highest scorer that night. In the last ten seconds I shot a three-point basket to win the game. The crowd **went wild.** Everyone was cheering so loudly I thought the roof of the gym would blow off. You'd think that my family would be proud. But no, it was just the usual pat on the head. My dad said, "Congratulations, kid."

Mom said, "You did a good job, Todd." And of course, John had to say something stupid. He said something about how terrible the gym smelled. But I knew I could count on Karen. And sure enough, she suggested we get ice cream.

I remember we passed the award case in the school's main hall. I've got quite a few awards in there. My latest one was for track and field. Karen hadn't seen it yet, so I pointed it out to her. She didn't even get a chance to say anything before Dad **butted in.** He said, "Karen, did you know John made the honor roll this term?"

My mom put her arms around John like she was going to hug him to death. She said, "We're so proud he's taking advanced science and western studies courses this year."

Hello everybody, do you remember me? I'm your other son. Are you unable to see me? I know everybody thinks that I'm an idiot. I know they think that John is a genius, but do they have to rub it in so much? Do they have to remind me of it every two seconds?

Well, everybody finally stopped gushing over John. Then we made our way out to the parking lot. As we got closer to the car, I noticed John was walking kind of fast. I figured he was trying to get to the car first and get a window seat. And I knew my parents would make me let Karen have the other window. That would mean I'd be **stuck** in the middle. No way, I thought. I'm not being crushed to death all the way to the ice cream parlor. So I started walking faster, too. John sped up. He was just about to reach the car door when I sped up and brushed past him. I guess it had rained during the game because the ground was wet and slippery. I swear I didn't touch John. But just as I got ahead of him, I heard a loud thump. I turned around and there was John on the ground. He was hollering like a baby. Everybody made a huge fuss over him. Mom said, "Todd, give your brother a hand."

I reached out to help John up, and he **scooted** into the car. Before I could say anything, he slid over to the window. Karen was standing behind me. So I had no choice but to get in the car and sit in the middle.

We finally got to the ice cream parlor and Karen told us her news. She said that she was engaged to a boy she met at college. They were going to be married after they graduated in June. Everybody started talking at once—about a church wedding and a honeymoon in Paris, France. I couldn't believe how quickly Karen and my parents had agreed on everything. All I could think was that Karen was leaving us for good. I guess my parents realized it, too, because Mom started crying. Dad looked like he wanted to cry, too. To tell you the truth, my throat felt a little tight and my eyes were stinging. I watched John calmly slurping down his milkshake. I said to myself, "Why can't he be the one to get married and leave the house?"

Karen looked at me and said, "What did you say, Todd?"

"Oh, nothing," I said. "Just that I'll miss you after you leave." Karen smiled and patted my arm. Mom suddenly got all businesslike.

"Well," she said. "I am not looking forward to cleaning out Karen's room."

It got quieter because John stopped hosing up his milkshake for two seconds. He said, "Don't worry Mom, I'll help you."

I looked over at John. What was he up to? Then Karen said, "I guess my room will be up for grabs after the wedding."

"That's it!" I thought to myself. "John thinks he can cheat me out of Karen's bedroom." It's bigger than ours and closer to the bathroom. "Well, John can think again. That bedroom is mine. I'm the oldest, and it's only fair that I should get it. For the last fifteen years of my life John has gotten everything I wanted. But he is not getting Karen's bedroom." Then I said to my mom, "I'll help you clean it out, too." John looked me straight in the eye and slurped up his milkshake. He was playing it cool. But I was just as capable to play it cool. I smiled at him and thought, "This is war, brother, war."

 Do you think Todd will get Karen's bedroom? Circle your answer.

Yes   No

Then keep reading to find out what takes place.

For the rest of the year I did everything I could think of to get Karen's bedroom. The first thing I did was tell my parents I wanted it. I told them it was only fair, since I was the oldest and deserved it. But all they would say was, "We haven't decided what is going to happen to Karen's room. We'll just have to wait and see."

That's when it hit me. If I was going to get Karen's bedroom I had to do more than try to make myself look good. I had to make John look bad. I know that sounds pretty rotten, but this was war. Soon I came across the perfect chance to get John in trouble.

Our parents are very strict about when to be home. If they say you have to be home by nine o'clock, you better be home by nine o'clock. Like my dad always says, "Nine o'clock doesn't mean nine-thirty. It doesn't mean a quarter past nine, either. It means nine o'clock."

It used to make me groan just thinking about my dad saying that. But now it brought a smile to my face. I actually rubbed my hands together like a movie bad guy as I pictured my dad yelling at John. I could see my mother in the background. She had her hand on her forehead and she was saying, "How could you do this to us John?"

It was a Saturday, and my parents were going to have dinner at Brian's house that night. That's Karen's boyfriend. Our parents were meeting Brian's parents for the first time. The next week they were coming to our house for dinner. Mom and Dad were upstairs getting ready to leave when the phone rang. I answered, and it was John. He was calling from his science club, the "Astronuts." That's not the real name of the club. But that's what I call it. It's a bunch of kids from school who have nothing better to do than look up at the sky, point at stars, and say "Oh! Ah!" Boring!

Anyway, John told me to tell our parents that the club was going to let out two hours later than usual. They were expecting two planets to run into each other or something. I told him I'd pass the message on. He was so happy to get back to his fellow "Astronuts" that he just said "thanks" and hung up. Mom and Dad came downstairs. They were both so nervous and excited about meeting Brian's family. Even if I had given them John's message, I don't think they would have heard me. They said they'd be home at eleven. "Good," I thought. "That's a whole half hour before John will get home."

I was eating snacks and watching TV. Then, around nine o'clock, John comes home. "What are you doing here? You're supposed to be looking for aliens!" I said.

"I'm supposed to be watching a meteor shower," said John in a snooty voice. "And even you should know you can't do that in the rain."

He was right. It was pouring rain outside. I guess I'd been so caught up in the movie that I didn't even notice. Great! Even the weather was on John's side. But I wasn't ready to give up. Not yet.

The next Friday morning I got up for school and went down for breakfast as usual. But the house was very quiet. Then I noticed a note in the kitchen:

Boys—I had to go out to the store. There has been a change of plans. Brian's family is coming for dinner tonight at six o'clock. I want you both to come home right after school. Remember, this is a very important night for Karen. Your lunches are in the refrigerator. I'll see you later.

Love,

Mom

I thought, "Boy would John get in trouble if he didn't get home in time." I knew that he was planning to go to the river after school with another club of his. He'd be filthy when he came home. I could just see the look on Mom's face when John came in around six o'clock covered in mud. There was no way John would get Karen's room after ruining this dinner!

I wrote out a new note from Mom saying only that she was at the store, and that our lunches were in the refrigerator. Then I heard John coming downstairs, so I hid in the laundry room. I heard him open the refrigerator and get his lunch. Soon I heard him leave. I grabbed the note I had written, then put Mom's note back. Everything was falling into place.

The only problem was that I kept thinking about my mom's note. All day at school it was as if I could hear her saying, "Remember, this is a very important night for Karen." By the end of the day I was a total wreck. When the final bell rang, I ran to John's classroom and told him we had to get home right away. It was a great plan, but I just couldn't do it.

I was pretty discouraged, but I wasn't about to give up. I did all my chores without any complaining. I even did them before my parents could remind me, but so did John. We actually got into a terrible fight about whose turn it was to do the dishes. In the past, the fight had always gone, "It's your turn, not mine." This time I knew it was really John's turn. But I was arguing that it was my turn to do the dishes! The sneak actually let me win! And wouldn't you know, he still got to look good for not wanting to fight.

That's how things kept going. When I offered to take out the garbage, John invented a new recycling system. When John took over my mom's garden, I offered to mow the lawn for my dad. It wasn't my fault the lawn mower broke. Of course, John fixed the lawn mower and finished mowing the lawn. No matter what I did, I just couldn't seem to catch a break.

Finally, it was the day of the wedding. In between crying and hugging, Mom and Karen were getting ready. Dad was running around looking for the camera and blowing his nose. I was alone in the bedroom I shared with John. I was glad that John wasn't there. I could practice knotting my tie without him laughing at me. All of a sudden I noticed that some of the plants for one of his precious experiments were missing. I thought, "What's going on?" Then I began to wonder where he was. I decided to look for him. I stepped out into the hall and heard a noise coming from Karen's room. The door was slightly open and I stepped inside.

I couldn't believe what I saw. There was John setting up his plants in Karen's room. "You little sneak!" I yelled.

"What's your problem?" said John.

"My problem is that you're trying to steal Karen's room."

"I'm just putting some plants in here."

"Oh, no you're not," I said. I walked over to the plants. John tried to block me, but I stepped around him. Then I picked up one of his plants to take back to our room. John told me to stop and tried to grab the plant out of my hand. I pulled away from him. The plant slipped to the floor and its container broke. Dirt and the plant spilled all over the floor. John went crazy. I had never seen him so angry. He jumped on me and knocked me to the floor. We were grunting and rolling around like we were trying out for the school wrestling team. The way it was going, John seemed like he had a good chance of making first string.

Suddenly the bedroom door opened. "What is going on in here?"

John and I rolled apart. I rubbed the dirt out of my eyes and looked up into my sister's face. Karen was wearing her wedding dress and looked beautiful. She also looked mad. ▶

You Be The Judge

◆ 1. Do you think Todd should get the bedroom? Why or why not? Write what you think on the lines below.

_____

_____

2. What would be a fair way to decide who gets the room? Write what you think on the lines below.

_____

_____

Think About the Story

Use Story Words

◆ **Directions:** Look at your list of story words on page 101. Write a story word on each line.

3. John's idea of fun is looking at _____ under a microscope.

4. Karen will honeymoon in _____.

5. Todd's name is always in the sports _____ of the school newspaper.

6. John _____ a science class in summer school.

7. Todd's brother is taking a class in _____ studies.

Write Sentences About the Story

◆ **Directions:** Use words from the story to answer these questions.

8. What are John and Todd's different ideas of fun?

_____

_____

_____

9. Why did John repeat a science class in summer school?

_____

_____

_____

10. Why does Todd want Karen's bedroom?

_____

_____

The Big Idea

11. Which sentence tells what the whole story is about? Circle it.

    a. Todd calls his brother "nerds."

    b. Todd and John both want Karen's bedroom.

    c. Karen is getting married.

Words and Meanings

◆ **Directions:** Think about how the **bold** words are used in the story. Then circle the words that show the meaning of each word or phrase.

12. The crowd **went wild.** What does this mean?

    a. The crowd turned into animals.

    b. The crowd went to a place called Wild.

    c. The crowd got very excited.

13. Dad **butted in.** What does this mean?

    a. Dad said, "But."

    b. Dad interrupted the conversation.

    c. Dad bumped into Todd and Karen.

14. Todd did not want to be **stuck** in the middle of the backseat. What does this mean?

    a. Todd did not want to be glued to the seat.

    b. Todd did not want to be pushed into the car.

    c. Todd did not want to have to sit in the middle of the backseat.

15. John **scooted** into the car. What does this mean?

    a. John moved quickly into the car.

    b. John was riding a scooter.

    c. John looked into the car.

Look Ahead

◆ 16. What will Karen say to her brothers? Write what you think on the lines below. Then read on to find out if you are right.

_____

_____

Letters and Sounds

> **TIP:** The sound made when two vowels glide together in the same syllable to make a single sound is called a **diphthong**. A diphthong can appear at the beginning, the middle, or the end of a word. The vowel combinations **ai, ay, oi, oy**, and **ou** are diphthongs.

◆ **Directions:** Read the word. Write it on the line. Then circle all the diphthongs.

1. maintain _____

2. disappointment _____

3. mountain _____

4. playful _____

5. annoyingly _____

6. rejoice _____

7. bountifully _____

8. boisterously _____

◆ **Directions:** The diphthongs **oi** and **oy** make the same sound. They sound like the **oi** and **oy** in **oil** and **boy.** Read the words. Choose **oi** or **oy** to compete the word. Write it on the line.

9. b _____ l

10. t _____

11. _____ ster

12. f _____ l

13. c _____ l

14. c _____

15. br _____ l

16. f _____ er

17. s _____ l

18. t _____ l

19. dec _____

20. destr _____

21. enj _____

22. av _____ d

23. j _____ n

24. depl _____

25. rej _____ ce

Story Words

◆ **Directions:** Read each word to yourself. Then say the word out loud. Write the word on the line. Check the box after each step.

26. chemistry   Read ❑ Say ❑ Write ❑ _____
    (chem | is | try)

27. trophy (tro | phy)   Read ❑ Say ❑ Write ❑ _____

28. celebrate   Read ❑ Say ❑ Write ❑ _____
    (cel | e | brate)

29. cultivate   Read ❑ Say ❑ Write ❑ _____
    (cul | ti | vate)

More Word Work

◆ **Directions:** The suffixes **ous, eous,** and **ious** are found at the end of many words. Read the words. Write them on the lines. Circle the suffixes.

30. humorous   _____

31. beauteous   _____

32. gracious   _____

33. dangerous   _____

34. spacious   _____

35. marvelous   _____

36. mountainous   _____

37. perilous   _____

38. horrendous   _____

39. hideous   _____

40. envious   _____

Use What You Know

Part 1 of this story was told through Todd. Part 2 is John's story. How do you think the boys will differ in their views? Write what you think on the lines below.

_____

_____

_____

_____

BLOOD BROTHERS, PART 2

Maybe you think what I did was wrong. After all, it was my own brother I was fighting. I can understand if you think I was wrong. Believe me, I'm prepared to accept that. But, as the old saying goes, there are two sides to every story. Here's my side of the story.

Ever since I can remember, Todd has always **made a big deal** of the fact that he is older than I am. I would point out that he is only older by a year. He would always say, "Yeah John, but I'm still older than you are. And I'm bigger. I'm also faster and stronger than you are."

I have to admit everything he said was true. He was great at everything. I am hopeless at every sport ever invented. I finally got tired of losing every race we ran together. I got tired of looking like a fool when I struck out at baseball. I got tired of tripping over my own feet when we played basketball. So I stopped playing sports and got interested in nature and science instead. Even so, I still couldn't get away from the fact that Todd was the family star.

My parents would never admit that they like Todd better, but it's true. Actually, I don't blame them. It's pretty hard not to like Todd better than me. He's more exciting than I am. He hits a home run or scores a basket, and everybody cheers. Nobody cheers because you've memorized the names of all the elements for chemistry. They don't cheer because you're good at grammar. They don't care if you know the difference between a suffix and a prefix, either. It wouldn't have been so bad if I wasn't reminded all the time how great my brother was, but everything was about Todd. Mom was always putting out a new trophy Todd had just won. Dad was always talking about a race where Todd had just finished first. Sometimes I would complain about having to spend every second of my life at games where Todd was competing. Whenever I objected my mother would say, "Don't be fresh," and my dad would say, "Where's your family spirit?"

I was there the time Todd won the big school basketball game. Our whole family was there. Even our sister Karen had come home from college. Todd won the game almost all by himself. The whole school was cheering for him. Karen and my parents couldn't stop telling him how great he was. I never know what to say at those times. I just stand around. I hang my head and look at my shoes. I'm not jealous. I just feel like such a phony slapping Todd on the back and saying, "Great job, kid." Usually I would try and make some kind of a joke. I said, "The better the game is the worse the gym smells." Todd just looked at me like I was from Mars.

Todd didn't want us to forget how wonderful he is, so he dragged all of us over to the school's award case. He's won almost every trophy in there. Everybody gushed over him for about an hour. I guess my parents started to feel bad for me. My mom put a fake smile on her face and said, "John, tell everybody about your science classes." Then Dad jumped in saying how proud he is of all his kids.

I hate when they do that. It only makes me feel worse. I know they're all thinking, "Poor John, he's such a disappointment compared to his brother." I was feeling pretty down that night. I just wanted to go home, but I still had to watch the family celebrate at the ice cream shop. How was I supposed to eat and listen to Todd bragging at the same time? It would be a miracle if I didn't get sick.

We left the school and headed out to the car. I wanted to be by myself for a minute. I was walking a little faster than everybody else. Before I knew what was happening, Todd ran up and pushed me to the ground. I couldn't believe it. He's always doing things like that. Everybody acts like it's just fun and games. Well, it may be a game to them, but it's not fun for me. Then, Todd reached down to help me up. He was acting like he was coming to my rescue, like he was a big hero or something. I was so mad I just pulled away from him and got in the car.

All the way to the ice cream shop I thought about my life. My future looked pretty bleak. I knew I'd be standing in Todd's shadow for the rest of my hideous life. I felt like I couldn't take it anymore.

That night, my older sister Karen said something that gave me hope. She told us she was going to get married and leave home. Suddenly I realized I had the solution to my problems. I could move into Karen's old room and finally have a place to myself. Karen's room was the perfect place to grow some plants I wanted to cultivate. Her room faced south and got more sunlight than ours did. I could make a small greenhouse in there. Maybe I could even build a small lab. I could do some serious work. I could find the cure for the common cold. I could find the cure for cancer! I just knew I could do it. Then everything would be different. I wouldn't just be Todd's kid brother anymore. I'd be on television and in the newspapers. I'd be famous. Finally I'd be the one everyone cheered for.

I was so excited I almost asked my parents for the room right then and there. But I knew that would be a mistake. The minute I said I wanted it, Todd would want it, too. So when my mom said Karen's room would need cleaning out, I told her I'd help. Then Todd said he'd help also. He never volunteers to do anything. My **heart sank**. I knew he wanted the room. No, he didn't really want the room. He just didn't want me to get it. He was grinning at me. I knew he was thinking, "Too bad little brother."

I was madder than I've ever been in my life. I decided right then and there that Todd was not going to get Karen's bedroom. That room was mine. No matter what I had to do I was going to get it. It wasn't just for me. It was important for the world. Just think of all the people I would cure with my work. For once in his life, Todd would not win.

Do you think John will get the bedroom? Circle your answer.

Yes   No

Then keep reading to find out what takes place.

The more I thought about it, the more I realized that it wasn't Todd who stood between Karen's bedroom and me. It was my parents. Todd was a big pain all right, but he wasn't the problem. The problem was getting my parents to think that I should be the one to get the bedroom.

I decided to look at the problem like a scientist. I remembered stories about how companies used to get people to buy hot dogs and soda while they were watching a movie. The stories told how a picture of popcorn or somebody drinking a cold soda would be put right into the movie. But the picture of the food went by so quickly—it didn't even last a second—that the people didn't even know they had seen it. Only somewhere deep inside their mind did they know it. After the food was shown in the movie, people would get up to buy food.

I thought about taking a video and putting pictures into it. I'd put in my report card with straight A's. I'd put in the note from Todd's teacher saying she was sorry to hear my mother's father had died—Grandpa isn't dead. Todd just said that to get out of taking a test. Boy did he get in trouble! I'd also put in pictures of me taking out the garbage and washing my dad's car. Then I'd have pictures of Todd. There would be a picture of him standing at the open refrigerator, drinking milk right out of the carton. Mom hates when he does that. Another picture would show Todd fooling around with my father's golf clubs. He's not supposed to do that. And the last picture would show Todd's side of the bedroom. All you would be able to see was Todd's unmade bed and a huge pile of dirty clothes.

I could just imagine the whole family watching the movie together. After the places where I put in pictures of Todd, my parents would get mad. They'd start to yell at him. Todd wouldn't know what was going on. Then the really quick pictures of me being a perfect son would go by. My parents would turn to me, they'd say, "John, you are such a great kid. We think you should get Karen's bedroom." Yeah, that would be how I could get what I want.

But let's face it, there's no way I could put pictures into a video. Even if I could, I didn't know how to get pictures of myself doing those things. I couldn't exactly say, "Todd, take a picture of me washing Dad's car." Still, I wasn't ready to give up on the whole idea yet. I began to think that if you could change people with pictures, maybe you could also change people with sound.

I had also heard stories about how in wartime people have used loud music to harm an enemy. Any music will do, but if you play something your enemy hates, it's even better. So I set up a little project. I told my family I was doing an experiment to see how different kinds of music would affect plants. I put the plants in the dining room next to my CD player. I stacked up a whole bunch of CDs to play to the plants.

I started to hang out with my parents in the dining room. Sometimes I would just be with my mom. Sometimes I would just be with my dad. Sometimes all three of us would be together. At those times I would play music I know my parents love. You could just look at them and see them relax. They'd smile and sway a little to the music. Whenever Todd would come in I'd make an excuse about having to leave. But first I would change the music. I'd put on something loud and very screechy. My parents would start to cover their ears; they'd twist in their seats and soon get up and leave. Even Todd didn't look too happy. I'm not so sure the music had any effect on the plants but it sure had an effect on my family!

The idea was that my parents would have good feelings around me and bad feelings around Todd. They would start to dislike him and wouldn't want to do anything nice for him. Then naturally they'd want me to get Karen's room. Well, it was a great idea, but it didn't work out the way I had hoped. My parents just told me to move my experiment to the basement. So just like Todd, I was back to begging them and trying to please them.

The day of Karen's wedding, I was feeling pretty low. I was alone in our bedroom. I was thinking about all the months since Karen told us she was getting married. I had done everything I could think of to get on my parent's good side. I'm always helpful. But lately I had been especially helpful. But so had Todd. And I knew that they were more impressed by him. He never used to do anything around the house, so of course they noticed it more when he started helping. It didn't matter that I worked much harder than Todd. It was like I wasn't there.

Later, I sat on my bed and looked around the room. I looked at Todd's trophies and medals all over the place. I looked at my plants crowded together under the window. They weren't doing well. They needed more space and light. That was when I decided to move them. I wasn't trying to be sneaky. I just wanted to give my plants a chance to grow.

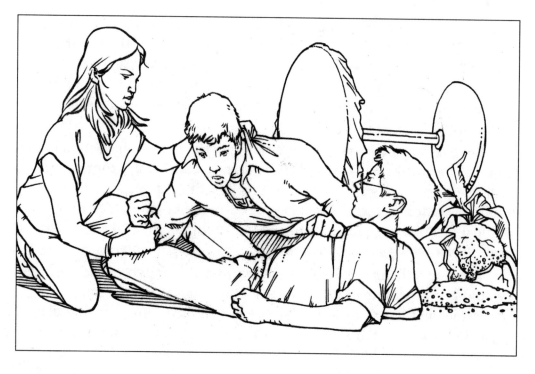

I had just moved a few of the plants into Karen's room when Todd burst in the door. He started yelling at me and calling me names. Then he did something that really made me mad. He said it was an accident. To me it looked like he just grabbed one of my plants and threw it on the floor. The pot broke. I got so mad I really did see red. I jumped on Todd. We fell to the floor. We began rolling around in the dirt and broken pottery pieces.

Suddenly Karen was in the room. She pulled us apart. Todd yelled out, "John was trying to steal your room."

"That's not true."

"Quiet!" said Karen. "I don't want to hear another word. Look at the two of you. You're filthy and you're bleeding!"

"Yeah, well, Todd—"

"Just be quiet," she said.

"Yeah, John—"

"You too, Todd. I don't want to hear a word from either of you. You don't know how lucky you are. All my life I wished I had a sister. When you were little you two were so close. You were always together. You were always laughing. Now look at you, covered in dirt and bleeding. The last time you were both bleeding was when you decided to become blood brothers. Do you remember that? You'd seen some movie where two friends cut themselves and mixed their blood together. Mom was mad. She said you were already blood brothers. But you said you just wanted to make sure. What happened to those two brothers? What happened to those two friends?"

I started to remember all the times Todd stood up for me at school. I remembered how he let me teach him the names of all the planets and stars. I remembered how he always picked me first to play on his team, even though I was the worst player in the world. I remembered all the fun we used to have, and I felt pretty bad. I guess Todd did too, because he wiped some blood off my arm. He wiped some of his own blood from under his nose. Then he mixed our blood together. He said, "I guess we're still blood brothers."

We didn't get mushy or anything. There was no time for that anyway. We had to hurry and get cleaned up and changed for Karen's wedding. We got there just in time, and it was great. All the grownups said it was a beautiful wedding, which is what they always say. But I think Karen's really was. We laughed almost the entire day. The whole family had a great time.

By the way, neither Todd nor I got Karen's old bedroom. Our parents decided to turn it into a family room. We still share a bedroom, but we don't mind it so much anymore.

You Be the Judge

1. Karen said that John and Todd used to be close friends. She wants to know why they are always fighting now. Why do you think they fight more now? Write what you think on the lines below.

_____

_____

_____

_____

Think About the Story

Use Story Words

Directions: Look at your list of story words on page 111. Write a story word on each line.

2. A birthday party is held to _____ someone's birth.

3. A greenhouse is a perfect place to _____ plants.

4. The winner of a race may win a _____ or a medal.

5. John did a lot of memorization for his _____ class.

When Did It Happen?

6. Write a number from 1 to 4 in front of each event to show when it happened.

_____ Karen told the boys to stop fighting.

_____ John put his plants in Karen's bedroom.

_____ The family went to Todd's basketball game.

_____ John decides he wants Karen's bedroom.

What Are the Facts?

7. Why did John think his parents liked Todd better than him? Circle the reasons.

   a. They told him they did.

   b. John thinks Todd is more exciting than he is.

   c. John thinks his parents are always praising Todd.

   d. His parents gave Todd Karen's bedroom.

   e. His mother displays Todd's many trophies.

Write Sentences About the Story

◆ **Directions:** Use words from the story to answer these questions.

8. Why does John like nature and science instead of sports?

     _____

     _____

9. Why does John want to move into Karen's room?

     _____

     _____

10. Why does Todd say, "I guess we're still blood brothers"?

     _____

     _____

Words and Meanings

◆ **Directions:** Think about how the **bold** words are used in the story. Then circle the words that show the meaning of each word or phrase.

11. Todd has always **made a big deal** about being older than John. What does this mean?
    a. Todd has always played cards with John.
    b. Todd has always stressed that he is older.
    c. Todd is always buying and selling things.

12. John said, "My **heart sank.**" He means he _____.
    a. is having a heart attack
    b. has heartburn
    c. felt sad

Why Did It Happen?

◆ **Directions:** Draw a line from each story event to the reason it happened.

What Happened	Why
13. John moved his plants to Karen's room	○ because Todd dropped John's plant.
14. John offered to help his mom clean Karen's room	○ because they would grow better.
15. John pushed Todd down	○ in order to convince his parents to give him the room.

Chapter 2 Summary of Skills and Strategies

Let's look back at what you learned in Chapter 2.

Letters and Sounds

◆ You learned. . .

- the letter **g** has a **soft** sound and a **hard** sound.
- the letters **ough** and **augh** make different sounds.
- the long **e** vowel can be made with the letters **ie**.
- the **schwa** sound can be made by many letters and letter combinations.
- the sound of diphthongs such as **ai, ay, oi, oy,** and **ou.**

Words and Meanings

◆ You learned. . .

- the suffixes **ly, ful, less, ness, ment, y, able, ible, ous, eous,** and **ious.**
- how to use the suffixes **er** and **est** to compare two or more things.
- how to make compound words.
- how to make contractions.

Stories and Skills

◆ You learned. . .

- how a high school student learns to choose friends wisely.
- how two brothers stop fighting long enough to discover the strength of their friendship.
- how dog guides and their partners train and work together.
- how students volunteer to help other people.

◆ You learned. . .

- how to use what you know to help you understand stories.
- how to predict what story characters might do.
- how to use questions about what you are reading to help your understanding.

The chapter review will give you a chance to show what you have learned.

Part A

Summing It Up: Letters and Sounds

▶ The letter **g** has a **soft sound,** as in the word **gym.**

▶ The letter **g** also has a **hard sound,** as in the word **good.**

◆ **Directions:** Read each word. Write an **S** on the line after the words that have a **soft g.** Write an **H** on the line after the words that have a **hard g.**

1. gold _____
2. ginger _____
3. ago _____
4. village _____
5. gem _____

6. get _____
7. judge _____
8. government _____
9. pig _____
10. germ _____

▶ The letters **ough** can have the sound of the letter **o** in the word **lost,** as in **thought.**

▶ The letters **ough** can have the sound of the letters **ou** in the word **out,** as in **plough.**

▶ The letters **ough** can have the sound of the letter **u** in the word **cut,** as in **rough.**

▶ The letters **augh** can have the sound of **aw** in the word **saw,** as in **naughty.**

▶ The letters **augh** can have the sound of **af** in the word **staff,** as in **laugh.**

◆ **Directions:** The letters **ough** appear in many words. Write the letters below on the lines. See how many words you can make.

c	en	f	l	r	s	t

11. _____ ough
12. _____ ough
13. _____ ough
14. _____ ough
15. _____ augh

16. _____ ought
17. _____ ought
18. _____ aught
19. _____ aught

- The letter pair **ie** makes the long **e** vowel sound.
- The letter pair **ei** follows the letter **c** and makes the long **a** vowel sound.
- The letter pair **ei** can stand for the long **e** sound, but only if the letter **c** sounds like **s**, as in **glacier.**
- A rhyme that helps you remember is: Use **i** before **e** when sounded like **ee,** except after **c,** or when sounded like **a,** as in **neighbor** and **weigh.**

Directions: Read the words. They are missing the letters **ei** or **ie.** Write the correct letter pair to complete the words. Write the complete word on the line.

20. c _____ ling _____

21. y _____ ld _____

22. th _____ f _____

23. rec _____ pt _____

24. rel _____ ve _____

25. v _____ n _____

- The sound of the letter **a** in **ago** is called the **schwa** sound.
- The vowels **a, e, i, o,** and **u** can all stand for the **schwa** sound.
- The letter patterns **el, al, le, er, or, ar, en, on, ed, id,** or **ion** can all stand for the **schwa** sound.
- The **schwa** is usually in an unstressed part of the word.

Directions: Write the word on the line. Circle the schwa sounds in the words.

26. company _____   34. able _____

27. suppose _____   35. mechanical _____

28. horrible _____   36. shower _____

29. position _____   37. inspection _____

30. hasten _____   38. capable _____

31. spectacular _____   39. cereal _____

32. person _____   40. portable _____

33. terrible _____   41. creation _____

> ▶ The sound made when two vowels glide together in the same syllable to make a single sound is called a **diphthong**. Examples are the **oi** sound in **foil** or the **ou** sound in **horrendous**.
>
> ▶ A diphthong can appear at the beginning, the middle, or the end of a word.
>
> ▶ The vowel combinations **ai, ay, oi, oy,** and **ou** are diphthongs.

◆ **Directions:** Read the word. Write it on the line. Then circle all the diphthongs.

42. rainstorm   _____

43. horseplay   _____

44. appointment   _____

45. enjoyment   _____

46. resounding   _____

47. voiceover   _____

◆ **Directions:** Complete the words below with either **oi** or **oy**. Write the word on the line.

48. j _____   _____

49. br _____ ler   _____

50. f _____ er   _____

51. t _____ ling   _____

52. c _____   _____

Part B

Summing It Up: More Word Work

> ▸ The endings **er** and **est** can be added to adjectives to make them compare one thing to one or more other things.
>
> ▸ An adjective that ends in **er,** also called a **comparative** adjective, compares two things.
>
> ▸ An adjective that ends in **est,** which is called a **superlative** adjective, compares more than two things.

◆ **Directions:** Choose the correct word for the sentences below. Write the word on the line.

1. A mansion is (largest/larger) than a house. _____

2. A cat is bigger than a mouse, but a dog is the (biggest/bigger) of all three. _____

3. A church is (quieter/quietest) than an amusement park.

   _____

4. A handbag is (smallest/ smaller) than a suitcase.

   _____

5. The Empire State Building was once the (tallest/taller) building in the world. _____

6. A mountain is (greatest/greater) than a molehill.

   _____

7. Easy-listening music is (soft/softer) than rock and roll.

   _____

8. The sun is (brightest/brighter) than a flashlight. _____

> ▸ A **compound word** is made by putting together two words.
>
> ▸ A compound word has a new meaning that is different from the words that make it.
>
> ▸ Compound words are made in different ways. They are joined by a space, by a hyphen, or by no space at all. Examples are **fire station, fire-eater,** and **firefighter.**

◆ **Directions:** Choose a word from the list to make compound words on the lines below. Write out the new compound words.

shoe	house	works	home	table	time
hair	neck	glass	ball	watch	yard

9. work _____

10. day _____

11. fire _____

12. lace _____

13. foot _____

14. time _____

15. cut _____

16. hold _____

17. wrist _____

18. eye _____

19. barn _____

20. tie _____

▶ Contractions are made by joining together two words.
▶ Contractions use an apostrophe (') to mark letters that are dropped when the words are joined.

◆ **Directions:** Make a contraction of the words. Write it on the line.

21. I am _____

22. can not _____

23. would not _____

24. we will _____

25. it is _____

26. we would _____

27. could have _____

28. she will _____

29. he would _____

Part C

Story Words

♦ **Directions:** On the lines below, write the word from the list that matches each clue.

army	observe	astronomy	rhythm
column	particular	telescope	

1. a branch of the military _____

2. to watch closely _____

3. the study of outer space _____

4. a row _____

5. a steady sound or movement _____

6. a device for seeing things far away _____

7. something specific _____

♦ **Directions:** Select a word from the list to finish the sentence. Write the word on the line.

repeated   conference   gestured   Paris   planets   disappointed

8. Mars is one of the _____ in our solar system.

9. She _____ for Bill to sit down.

10. The Eiffel Tower is in _____.

11. Because they couldn't hear her, she _____ the directions.

12. The teacher and Ann's parents had a _____.

13. The coach was _____ with the loss.

♦ **Directions:** Read each word. On the lines below, write a number to tell how many syllables it has.

14. molecules _____   17. cultivate _____

15. southern _____   18. particular _____

16. boredom _____

◆ **Directions:** On the lines below, write the word from the list that matches each clue.

trophy	**yellow**	**partner**	**pedestrian**	**permanent**
property	**bonus**	**chemistry**	**western**	

19. the color of a banana _____

20. the science dealing with chemicals _____

21. lasting forever _____

22. an award or prize _____

23. the opposite of eastern _____

24. an added benefit _____

25. a helper or friend _____

26. land _____

27. someone who is walking _____

Part D

Think About the Stories

Fiction or Nonfiction?

◆ **Directions:** Write **fiction** next to the stories that were made up by the writer. Write **nonfiction** next to the stories that tell about real life.

1. "Finding New Friends"   _____

2. "Second Sight"   _____

3. "Student Volunteer"   _____

4. "Blood Brothers"   _____

Who Did What?

◆ **Directions:** Answer each question with the name of a person from the stories in Chapter 2.

Todd	**Priya**	**Karen**
José	**John**	**Peter**

5. Who was good at sports? _____

6. Who waited by the door to let his friend back into school?

   _____

7. Who was getting married? _____

8. Who was interested in science? _____

9. Who did volunteer work for Habitat for Humanity?

   _____

10. Who broke school rules to impress a new friend?

    _____

Why Did It Happen?

◆ **Directions:** Draw a line from each cause in Column A to its effect in Column B.

Column A	Column B
11. Because the boys were throwing napkins,	○ to learn skills and help others.
12. Todd and John were fighting because	○ they had broken school rules.
13. The blind use dog guides	○ they upset the man at the pizza parlor.
14. Students volunteer their time	○ he thought he was funny and daring.
15. José admired Fearless because	○ to move through the world safely and freely.
16. José and Peter had to go to detention because	○ they both wanted their sister's old bedroom.

CHAPTER 3

Letters and Sounds

◆ **Directions:** The letters **ou, au,** and **aw** can all stand for the **broad o** sound in **wrong.** Read each word. Write the word on the line.

1. thoughtlessness _____
2. automatic _____
3. awkwardly _____

◆ **Directions:** Write the word on the line, then circle the letters that make the **broad o** sound.

4. daughter-in-law _____
5. thoughtfulness _____
6. Pawnee _____
7. launchpad _____
8. wrought _____
9. awesomely _____
10. automobile _____
11. sought _____
12. trauma _____
13. pawnbroker _____
14. thought _____
15. automatic _____

◆ **Directions:** Write the letters on the lines. How many words can you make?

| b | c | cl | fl | h | th | tr | d |

16. ____ ough
17. ____ ough
18. ____ ough
19. ____ ough
20. ____ ough
21. ____ awk
22. ____ ought
23. ____ ought
24. ____ ause
25. ____ ause
26. ____ aw
27. ____ aw
28. ____ aw
29. ____ aw
30. ____ aughty
31. ____ aunt

Story Words

Directions: Read each word to yourself. Then say the word out loud. Write the word on the line. Check the box after each step.

32. volcano (vol | ca | no) Read ❑ Say ❑ Write ❑ _____

33. destruction   Read ❑ Say ❑ Write ❑ _____
    (de | struc | tion)

34. ancient (an | cient) Read ❑ Say ❑ Write ❑ _____

35. benefit (ben | e | fit) Read ❑ Say ❑ Write ❑ _____

36. electricity   Read ❑ Say ❑ Write ❑ _____
    (e | lec | tric | i | ty)

More Word Work

Directions: The prefixes **mid** and **mis** are found at the beginning of many words. The prefix **mid** means **"at"** or **"near the middle."** The prefix **mis** means **"wrong."** Read the word. Write the word on the line.

37. midweek   _____

38. misspell   _____

39. midpoint   _____

40. mistake   _____

Directions: Choose the correct prefix, **mis** or **mid**, for each word. Write the word on the line.

41. night   _____

42. ship   _____

43. behave   _____

44. lands   _____

45. judge   _____

46. deed   _____

47. stream   _____

48. fortune   _____

Use What You Know

Volcanic eruptions are just one of the powerful forces of nature. What is the most powerful natural force that you have experienced? What was it like? Write about your experience on the lines below.

_____

_____

_____

_____

LAVA SPILL

As a young girl growing up on the Caribbean island of St. Vincent's, Cynthia remembered stories about the island's Soufriére volcano. She would listen with her huge eyes open wide as elders told about the death and destruction caused by the eruption of the volcano in 1902. The eruption happened years before she was born. But these stories were so real that Cynthia was afraid to **close her eyes** for days after hearing them. Even now, in her seventies, Cynthia still remembers the stories that recalled a day that started peacefully. It was washing day. In every yard, white sheets hung from laundry lines. Children played in gardens and neighbors talked over backyard fences. Suddenly the calm was disturbed by many loud explosions. They sounded like a gun firing over and over. The bright afternoon sky grew dark as night. When the gloom lifted, the people were stilled, and the white laundry sheets were covered in ash.

On the island of Martinique, Mount Pelée erupted in the same year with even more tragic results. At the time of the eruption, an election was in progress. The candidates competed with loud rumblings from the island's volcano as they made their speeches. These rumblings were so distressing that some people left the island. Others wishing to vote in the election remained. When Mount Pelée erupted, the number of dead reached almost 30,000. It was one of the most destructive volcanic eruptions of the 1900s.

Though both Soufriére and Mount Pelée are in the Caribbean, volcanoes are found in many places in the world. In the United States, Mount St. Helen's erupted in the state of Washington. The results were disastrous. The volcano had been showing signs of increased activity for months. People came from all over the world to witness the event. A party mood prevailed as t-shirts, mugs, and other things were sold to the crowd. Though the police attempted to set up "safe zones," many people ignored them and moved forward to get a closer look at the volcano. They misjudged its power.

On the morning of May 18, 1980, these onlookers got more than they bargained for. Mount St. Helen's erupted. A huge, black cloud rose from the volcano. The cloud moved rapidly. It trapped many people in its intense heat and covered the area with ash. Many people suffered burns. A number of people died from these burns or from the poisonous gases released by the volcano. The impact of this one eruption even changed our weather patterns for years afterward.

In ancient times, people created myths, or stories, to explain the power of volcanoes. The Greeks claimed that a god named Zeus wished to **even a score** between himself and a monster named Typhon. Zeus set Typhon on fire and buried him under Mount Aetna. According to the legend, the monster's powerful screams caused the mountain to burst. The Romans told of the god Vulcan setting up a blacksmith shop on the Greek Isle of Lemnos. There he violently fanned his fire and carelessly threw hot rocks into the air. "Volcano" was the name they gave to Vulcan's workshop. It is the word we use today to name the force of nature.

Even in modern times, there have been people who thought the power of volcanoes is due to magical forces. In Hawaii some people believe in a volcanic character named Madam Pele. There are people who claim to have seen her when she takes the form of an old or young woman and walks the earth. Stories tell of drivers stopping their cars to give a ride to a strange woman. The woman sometimes speaks to the driver, and sometimes she is silent. At some point during the ride the driver looks away from the passenger. When the driver turns back to speak to her, the strange woman has left.

There are also those who believe that Madam Pele rewards those who are good to others. She appears to them and warns of upcoming volcanic eruptions. Some have even said that her warning allowed them to flee a volcanic eruption. Others claim that Madam Pele has changed the lava flow from an active volcano. This allowed them to spare their home and property.

There are other stories about Madam Pele's terrible anger when she feels wronged. The volcanic eruption in Hawaii in December of 1935 is one such story. The story describes how after the eruption of Mauna Loa, lava flowed down its mountainside toward the town of Hilo. As you will learn later, scientists sometimes bomb a lava flow to change its course or to stop its flow. Officials decided to attempt a bombing of the eruption's lava flow in hopes of saving the town. Some Hawaiians feared that such a step would anger Madam Pele and they warned against doing it. Despite their warnings, the army provided planes to drop bombs on the lava flow. On December 27, the planes dropped their bombs. A few days later the lava flow stopped, sparing the town of Hilo. Though many were happy, others warned that Madam Pele would soon take her revenge.

A month later over Luke Field in Oahu, two army planes ran into each other. There were a total of eight men on board the planes at the time of the crash. Of the eight men, six of them had been involved in bombing the lava flow a month earlier. The only survivors of the accident were two men who had not been involved in bombing Madam Pele's volcano. Those who understand science and the laws of nature think the crash was just an accident. But those who believe in the volcano goddess are sure that this was an act of Madam Pele's revenge.

Today scientists study the natural causes of volcanoes. To understand this powerful force, it is necessary to know the structure of the earth. Earth is made up of three layers. The center is called the core; it is made up of nickel and iron. The middle layer, or mantle, is made of a semi-solid rocky material. The outermost layer is known as the crust and is made up of brittle rock. The earth's core is very hot. Currents of heat rise through the mantle, cooling off as they near the crust. These cooler currents then sink back down to the core. Once again they heat up and rise to the surface. This rising and falling pattern continues again and again. Over the course of time, this process shapes the surface of the earth. It causes the brittle crust to stretch and contract until it breaks up into pieces like a jigsaw puzzle. The pieces of this puzzle are called plates.

With all this activity going on inside the earth, these plates are in constant movement. The edges of the plates bump up against each other. One plate may be pushed under the edge of the other. Scientists believe that the part of the plate that is pushed underneath becomes so hot that it melts. The melted substance, known as magma, rises up through the edges of two plates to form a volcano. Not all volcanoes occur at the edges of two plates. The volcanoes that form the Hawaiian Islands are in the middle of a plate. Scientists say that these volcanoes rise over hot spots. These areas of heat rise up through the mantle and burst through the crust.

Because they are formed differently, volcanoes look different. For example, the slopes of Mount St. Helen's are made up of many layers of rock and lava to form a composite volcano. Composite volcanoes are the result of many eruptions that rise up in the shape of a cone and often reach great heights.

Dome volcanoes are sometimes found on the slopes, or within the craters, of composite volcanoes. Dome volcanoes are made from lava and are usually small and round in shape.

A caldera is a crater volcano. Calderas are formed when heat causes a great explosion. It creates a large bowl-like hole as it breaks through the crust. Its name comes from the Spanish word for cauldron. Looking into one is like looking into a hot bubbling pot or cauldron.

The Hawaiian Islands have formed from shield volcanoes, which are broad and have low slopes. At the time of eruption the lava is very fluid and **moves like lightning.** It flows long distances. This makes the broad, gentle slopes that cause them to look like an overturned shield.

There are also many different kinds of volcanic eruptions. Eruptions may be made up of gas, rocks, and lava. As big as a fireworks display, these eruptions are often deadly to human and animal life. Some volcanic eruptions come without warning, like the one on Mount Pinatubo. This volcano in the Philippines hadn't erupted for over 400 years. It took everyone by surprise. It was one of the biggest eruptions of the 1900s. Most volcanoes give plenty of warning. Volcanoes like Mount St. Helen's can rumble and spew rocks for months and years before actually erupting.

How do you think it would be possible to stop or slow the flow of lava from a volcanic eruption? Write what you think on the lines below. Then keep reading to find out what scientists have tried.

_____

_____

_____

_____

Because of the great dangers of volcanic eruptions, people have tried to create ways to stop the flow of lava. One way is using natural and human-made barriers. Sometimes hills, gullies, walls, and ditches have stopped lava flow. But there have also been times when the lava simply piled higher and higher, flowed over a barrier, and continued in the same direction. Experts who have experience using barriers against lava flow explain that the barriers must have a very wide base. They must also be made of thick and heavy material if the lava is not to break through.

Another way of fighting hot lava is to cool it with water. Pouring on water can help slow the lava as the cooling lava becomes heavy. Sometimes water can make the lava form a solid crust and stop it completely. The first time water was used against lava was in 1960 when the Hawaiian volcano Kilauea erupted. Lava flowed through the town of Kapoho, destroying many homes and offices. The fire department slowed the lava by spraying it with water. This gave people enough time to gather their belongings and flee their homes. The major problem of fighting lava this way is that it requires huge amounts of water.

Sometimes the outer part of a flowing river of lava will form a crust. This creates a tube that keeps the lava hot inside. It allows the lava to stay liquid for longer periods. The lava then flows much farther than it would otherwise. To stop it midstream, the roof of the lava tube is bombed. This makes a vent in the tube that cools the lava and slows its flow. This was first tried in Hawaii when Mauna Loa erupted in 1935. Some Hawaiians were upset that scientists were trying to stop the lava flow with bombs.

They believed that the way to stop lava flows was to make offerings to the volcano. The argument was never truly settled, because the eruption of Mauna Loa stopped for unknown reasons.

Volcanoes can be deadly, but they also benefit people and the planet itself. In Europe, ancient hardened lava has been used to make buildings, walls, and streets. The Dutch have used volcanic rubble to build barriers against the North Sea. All over the world, volcanic soil is some of the best for growing crops. Many people are grateful for the benefits of hot springs and for electricity created by the heat of volcanoes. Volcanic action also forms gold, silver, copper, zinc, lead, and diamonds. Lastly, volcanoes create some of the most beautiful landscapes in the world. For all these reasons, people continue to risk living near volcanoes.

From the ancient Greeks to the modern-day tourists who travel the world to view them, volcanoes have long **captured people's imagination.** Though sometimes destructive, their benefits are great and their beauty and power are awe-inspiring. Those who witness a volcanic eruption are often at a loss to describe the event. They remember the experience all their lives, however. The stories of what they have seen are eventually passed on from person to person.

You Be the Judge

◆ 1. Because of the many benefits, people continue to live and work near volcanoes. Do you believe the benefits outweigh the risks? Why or why not? Write what you think on the lines below.

_____

_____

_____

Think About the Story

Use Story Words

◆ **Directions:** Look at your list of story words on page 131. Write a story word on each line.

2. _____ people made up stories to explain the causes of volcanoes.

3. People have found ways to produce _____ from volcanic heat.

4. A _____ is a powerful force of nature.

5. The _____ caused by the eruption of Mount St. Helen's was tragic.

6. Though volcanoes are destructive, they are also a _____ to people.

Write Sentences About the Story

◆ **Directions:** Circle the word that best fits in each sentence.

7. It is a (mistake/disbelief) to think we know everything about volcanoes.

8. Mount St. Helen's (erupting/erupted) in 1980.

9. Our word volcano (be/comes) from a Roman myth.

10. The mantle is the (middle/midriff) layer of the earth.

The Big Idea

11. Which sentence tells what the whole story is about? Circle it.

    a. Volcanoes have killed many people.

    b. Volcanoes are a natural force that is both destructive and beneficial.

    c. Mount St. Helen's erupted in 1980.

Words and Meanings

◆ **Directions:** Think about how the **bold** words are used in the story. Then circle the words that show the meaning of each word or phrase.

12. When Cynthia says she was afraid to **close her eyes,** she means _____.

    a. she didn't want to blink

    b. she was afraid to go to sleep

    c. her eyes hurt

13. Volcanoes have **captured people's imagination.** This means _____.

    a. volcanoes give us nightmares

    b. volcanoes have destroyed people's imaginations

    c. people are fascinated by volcanoes

14. Zeus wanted to **even a score** with Typhon. This means Zeus _____.

    a. wanted to get back at Typhon

    b. wanted to play a game with Typhon

    c. thought they had made a mistake counting game points

15. Fluid lava **moves like lightning.** This means it _____.

    a. makes a lot of noise

    b. can give you an electric shock

    c. moves very fast

Letters and Sounds

◈ **Directions:** These words have the sound of the **or** in **fort.** Circle the letters that make this **or** sound.

1. fortunately
2. boardinghouse
3. fourteen
4. fluorescent

◈ **Directions:** These words have the sound of the **ar** in **barn.** The letters **ear, or,** and **ar** can all have this sound. Circle the letters that make this **ar** sound.

5. artfully
6. carnival
7. heartless
8. sorry

◈ **Directions:** These words have the sound of the **ar** in **share** in them. The letters **ear, ere, ar,** and **air** can all have this sound. Circle the letters that make this **ar** sound.

9. therefore
10. warily
11. unfairness
12. bearable

◈ **Directions:** These words have the sound of **ir** in **irritate.** The letters **ear, eer, ere, ir,** and **ier** can all have this sound. Circle the letters that make this **ir** sound.

13. tearfully
14. hemisphere
15. buccaneer
16. cavalier

◈ **Directions:** These words have the sound of **ur** in **fur.** The letters **ear, or, ir, er,** and **ur** can all have this sound. Circle the letters that make this **ur** sound.

17. earnestly
18. turbine
19. certainly
20. birdhouse
21. worthless

◈ **Directions:** Write each word below under the word that has the same vowel sound.

| sorrowful | afford | wearable | aboard | atmosphere |
| pouring | farmhouse | hearing | fairly | barely |

fortunately	artfully	therefore	tearfully
22._____	25._____	27._____	30._____
23._____	26._____	28._____	31._____
24._____		29._____	

Story Words

◆ **Directions:** Read each word to yourself. Then say the word out loud. Write the word on the line. Check the box after each step.

32. caseworker   Read ❑ Say ❑ Write ❑ _____
    (case | work | er)

33. peered   Read ❑ Say ❑ Write ❑ _____

34. routine (rou | tine) Read ❑ Say ❑ Write ❑ _____

35. necessary   Read ❑ Say ❑ Write ❑ _____
    (nec | es | sar | y)

36. allowance   Read ❑ Say ❑ Write ❑ _____
    (al | low | ance)

37. accusing   Read ❑ Say ❑ Write ❑ _____
    (ac | cus | ing)

More Word Work

A prefix is added to the beginning of a word. The prefix **sub** means "under." The prefix **trans** means "across."

Example: sub + marine = submarine (underwater)
            trans + continental = transcontinental (across the continent)

◆ **Directions:** These words have prefixes. Write the word on the line. Circle the prefix in each word. Tell what each word means.

38. subzero   _____ _____

39. transnational _____ _____

40. transport   _____ _____

41. subscript   _____ _____

42. subset   _____ _____

43. transmit   _____ _____

Use What You Know

Sandra leaves from the city to live with a foster family in the country. What do you know about life in the country? Is it different from life in the city? How? Write what you think on the lines below.

_____

_____

_____

FOSTER CHILD

Sandra stared out the window. The flat land and the road seemed to go on endlessly. She wasn't too happy about this trip. She was on her way to a foster home. It was a two-hour car ride from the city to her new home. Her new home was on a farm in the country. Her caseworker, Susan, was driving her there. Susan was always asking Sandra questions about her life. Sometimes Sandra just wanted to be left alone.

Sandra wanted to live with her own family. Her mother and father had problems and neither one could care for her. She was taken away for foster care. She missed her friends from her old neighborhood. They still lived with their families. Sandra and her friends used to hang around together. Sometimes they would stay out really late into the night. Her parents didn't notice that she wasn't at home.

The car pulled off the main road and onto a long, dirt and gravel driveway. As they rode up to the house, Sandra peered out the window again. This didn't look like the farms she had seen in books and on TV. There were no rows of corn growing in the fields. There were three large glass buildings instead of a barn with chickens and cows. The sign out front said "Groves Greenhouse." The Groves were her new "family."

The Groves came outside when the car pulled up. As they walked over, a large, brown barking dog came bounding down the steps. Mr. Grove whistled sharply. The dog stopped barking, then ran right up to Sandra and put his front paws on her shirt. She smiled and patted its head.

"Hello, Sandra," said Mr. Grove. "This is Jasper. We rescued him from the animal shelter about two years ago. We think he is part collie and part mutt! He is very friendly, as you can see."

Sandra didn't say anything. She continued to pet Jasper.

"I am Charlie and this is Amy Jo. We are happy to have you with us."

Sandra just stared at them. She didn't know what to say to country people. She was nervous and was glad that Jasper was there. She wished she were back at home. She was never at a loss for words there.

"Right. So, come on in and we'll show you around," said Amy Jo.

Susan had been to the farm before. She had to check it out to make sure Sandra could live there. She had said, "Nice to see you again," when they arrived. She told Sandra that she had met the Groves. She had to learn about them and to judge whether they would be good foster parents. Susan had given her approval.

Charlie told Sandra that the house was really an old farmhouse that they had restored. It was run-down when they bought it. However, it was attached to land that would be good for their business.

They walked up a curving, wooden staircase. Sandra's room was at the end of the hallway. It had a window that looked out on a yard with trees and flowers. The room had simple furniture and a small rug on the hardwood floor. Sandra didn't like that all three adults seemed to be looking at her, expecting something from her.

Charlie and Susan went down to get Sandra's things from the car. Amy Jo said, "I want to give you a tour of the farm. Why don't you relax here for a little while first? The car ride was long."

Sandra said, "Yeah." She never went on long car rides. She grew up in the city. Her family didn't go on vacations.

Charlie and Susan brought up her bag and her backpack. When Charlie left the room, Susan said that she would be leaving to go back to the city. She reminded Sandra that she had her phone number and to call if she wanted to talk. Susan said, "I think you'll like living on the farm. Give it a chance."

Amy Jo came back and led Sandra outside. "Do you go by Sandra or Sandy?" Amy Jo asked.

"Sandra," she replied. She only let her parents and friends call her Sandy.

"Okay, Sandra. Welcome to Groves Greenhouse. What we do is grow flowers and plants to sell to people and small businesses. We deliver large orders to our customers. They may also take their purchases home with them. We grow many kinds of flowers and other plants. Some of them are grown in the greenhouses,"—she pointed to the glass buildings—"and some are grown in the fields. All of our plants receive proper care, including watering and weeding."

Sandra had never seen so many kinds of plants in one place. She wondered how the Groves could keep track of all of them.

Amy Jo led Sandra into one of the greenhouses. It was warm inside. "The glass helps to keep in the warm air. It also lets the sun's rays get in easily and then traps the warmth inside." She pointed to one of the glass panes. It was open, like a window. "We have vents that allow the air to move around. We don't want it to get too hot in here. The plants need warmth, but not too much, because we don't grow many tropical plants."

Sandra decided that she wouldn't melt in the greenhouse, although **the air seemed sticky**. She looked around at the flowers and other plants. She decided that she wasn't interested in this business of the Groves. It was nothing like the people who sold flowers in the city.

Amy Jo continued to lead Sandra into each of the three greenhouses. Amy Jo pointed out plants that Sandra had never heard of before. The flowers were brightly colored, mixed in with the green of the leaves and stems. The air smelled good. Sandra could smell the flowers without getting close. The Groves also grew vegetables and many kinds of plants that Amy Jo called shrubs.

When they left the greenhouses, Amy Jo told Sandra about the plants in the fields. They had a system that watered the plants. The water was set on a timer so that the Groves didn't have to turn it on and off. When the plants grew larger, they would be transplanted.

After the tour, the Groves and Sandra ate dinner. They had homegrown vegetables with the meal. Sandra had to admit that they tasted good. She didn't usually have meals like this. When Amy Jo asked her if she enjoyed the meal, Sandra replied with "Yes!"

Sandra's first day drew to a close. She still went to bed feeling lonely, but the day had passed quickly. She lay in bed listening to the crickets. It was so quiet out here in the country. Sometimes she heard Jasper bark at some unknown creature. She missed the sounds of the people, cars, and sirens that she was used to hearing in the city.

The next morning Sandra was up early, at least for her. She found Charlie and Amy Jo already hard at work in the greenhouses. Amy Jo was cutting back some of the plants and removing dead flowers. Charlie was spraying something on the leaves of some of the plants. He said it was a

mix to help the plants grow. He said it would also keep some of the insects away. He handed Sandra a watering can. He pointed out the hose to her. She must have stared blankly at him because he told her to fill the watering can. After she filled it, she came back, and he told her which plants to water. Sandra did as she was told.

This became the morning routine. Each day she would spend the morning watering the plants. Sometimes she used a hose and sometimes she used the watering can. Sandra didn't realize that she would have to work for her foster parents. She wasn't happy about this at all. During summers at home, she hung around with her friends all day. In the city she didn't have to work.

Sometimes the Groves were visited by customers in search of plants for their garden. Charlie and Amy Jo would let them wander around, offering help when necessary. When someone wanted to buy something, they went to the cash register that was in the corner of one of the greenhouses. Charlie told Sandra that he would teach her how to use the cash register someday soon.

"Great," she thought. "More work."

One day, Jasper's barking marked the arrival of the Groves' accountant, Ray. The Groves had told Ray about Sandra, so he was not surprised to see her. He tried to **strike up a conversation** with her. "Are you enjoying yourself on the farm?" he asked.

Sandra shrugged her shoulders.

Ray seemed interested in Sandra's work. He asked her more questions about her life in the city. She gave him short answers and continued with her work. Ray and Charlie went into the house to discuss the **books.** Amy Jo was helping a customer on another part of the farm. Some workers were loading shrubs into a delivery truck that another customer had brought. Sandra decided that she needed a break.

She went for a walk around the farm, careful to avoid Amy Jo's eyes. She hid herself among the shrubs and sat down to think. She still missed the city and her friends. She thought country life was boring. There was no excitement. There were hardly any people around. There were no subways. "How do they have any fun?" she thought.

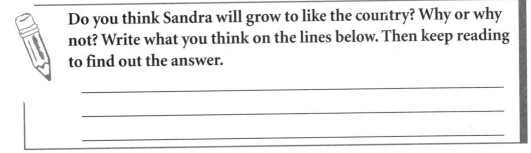

Do you think Sandra will grow to like the country? Why or why not? Write what you think on the lines below. Then keep reading to find out the answer.

_____

_____

_____

After a while, she returned to the greenhouse. Ray was leaving and Jasper was barking. "See you next time, old boy," Ray said to the dog.

That night, while they were eating dinner, Charlie told Sandra that she was doing a great job on the farm. Sandra was pleased. Amy Jo said that they really liked her work. She told Sandra to tell her if the work was too much for her. Sandra said that she would.

The next day, Amy Jo told Sandra that she had some news for her. Susan, her caseworker, had arranged for three of Sandra's friends to come visit. Amy Jo was going to pick them up from the bus station.

Sandra was excited, but also worried. She wondered what her friends would think of her new life. She hoped they wouldn't laugh at her for working on a farm. She hadn't seen them in a while. She hoped she hadn't been left out of too many things back home.

Sandra went with Amy Jo to pick up her friends, Cara, Jago, and Yolanda. Sandra and her friends hugged each other when they were reunited. As they drove back to the farm, Amy Jo told Sandra's friends about the business. She said it had been a good summer for the business. She was happy with the way things were going. She also praised Sandra for helping out in the greenhouses. Sandra felt good about her work.

When they returned, Sandra gave the girls a tour of the farm. She showed them how she watered the plants. She named a few of the plants for her friends. She tried to impress them. Yolanda asked her about what she did for fun on the farm. Sandra told her that it was pretty quiet. She said that she and Jasper went for long walks.

"Don't you get bored?" said Yolanda.

"Why do they make you work?" said Cara.

Sandra became defensive. "Well, there isn't that much time to be bored," replied Sandra. "Charlie and Amy Jo wanted to help me enjoy nature and some of the food we eat. Besides, they give me an allowance for helping out. I don't have to help. I like it." Sandra had admitted it. She enjoyed working in the greenhouse. She liked the routine of caring for the plants. It made her feel good to think that she was responsible for them.

The girls stayed in the greenhouse a while. In the afternoon, Ray came by and the girls went to play with Jasper. Sandra enjoyed showing him off as well. He and Sandra had both learned how to adjust to farm life.

It was time to drive the girls back to the bus station. Sandra was sorry to see them go, but she wasn't as sad as she once was. She told her friends to come back to visit. She hoped they would stay longer next time and learn more about the farm.

When Amy Jo and Sandra returned to the house, Sandra noticed that Charlie seemed a little out of sorts. He and Amy Jo went into the office to talk. Sandra went upstairs to her room to think about the day. She decided that she was glad that she came to live with the Groves. They seemed to care about her and they trusted her. They were different from her own parents.

Amy Jo and Charlie knocked on her door. "We need to talk to you," Charlie said.

"Oh, no," thought Sandra. Things had been going so well. She wondered what she did. Sandra opened the door and they came in.

"Sandra, were you and your friends in greenhouse number one today?" asked Charlie.

"Um, yes," Sandra stammered.

"Sandra, there is quite a bit of money missing from the cash register. I'm sorry to say we think your friends may have taken it."

Sandra gulped. "But they couldn't have. I was with them the whole day. I didn't see them anywhere near the cash register."

"Sandra, your friends are from the city. They have different ways from us country folk. We need to think about how we should handle this," said Charlie.

Sandra was disappointed. She knew her friends didn't take the money. She thought it was unfair of Charlie to blame them, just because they were from the city. He hadn't seen them take the money.

"I will pay you back for what is missing," said Sandra. "I will use the money from my allowance."

Charlie and Amy Jo looked at each other. "That's not necessary, Sandra," said Amy Jo. "Besides, your allowance would take a long time to pay it off. It's time for dinner," said Amy Jo. "Let's eat and we can talk about this later."

Dinner was almost silent. Sandra was very upset. It was almost as if they were accusing her of stealing. She made it through dinner and went straight to her room.

"Maybe I don't belong here," she thought. "How can I live here if they don't trust or believe me?"

The incident passed and nothing more was said. Sandra continued with her greenhouse duties. She didn't feel quite the same as before though.

One day a few weeks later, Sandra walked up to Greenhouse #1 from the field. She thought she noticed someone inside. She peered through the window through the leaves of a hanging fern.

Sandra was amazed to see Ray at the cash register. He was taking money out of it and stuffing it into his pockets! She was shocked. She couldn't move. Her **heart was racing.**

Sandra backed away from the greenhouse. She had to find Charlie. She ran as fast as she could. She found him in one of the rows in the field.

"Charlie," she panted, "I know who did it! I know who took the money! It was Ray!"

Charlie stared at her.

"I just saw him take money out of the cash register. He didn't know I was watching."

Charlie paused for just a second. "Come on." They went together to Greenhouse #1. Ray was standing outside. "Charlie, there you are. I was just getting ready to leave."

Charlie looked at Sandra, who returned his look with **pleading eyes.**

"Ray, I think we better have a talk." They went into the house and shut the door to the office. They came out ten minutes later. Ray walked to his car and left without looking back.

"What was that all about?" asked Amy Jo.

"I'm terribly sorry, Sandra," said Charlie. "Can you forgive us for accusing your friends of stealing? Ray told us that he saw your friends near the cash register. We've known Ray a long time, so I believed him. He won't be coming around here anymore. I'm sorry I was so quick to judge your friends."

"Thank you for believing me," said Sandra. She felt like **a great weight was lifted from her shoulders.** "Thank you," she said again.

That night, as she was preparing for bed, Charlie and Amy Jo walked down to say good night. "Good night, Sandra," said Charlie.

"You can call me Sandy," said Sandra.

In bed, she listened once again to the quiet sounds of the country. She smiled as she thought about herself as a country girl. The crickets and Jasper's quiet barks lulled her to sleep.

You Be the Judge

◆ 1. Sandra's caseworker took her away from the city to a new home in the country. Do you think taking a foster child to a different home is a good idea? Why or why not? Write what you think on the lines below.

_____

_____

Think About the Story

Use Story Words

◆ **Directions:** Look at your list of story words on page 141. Write a story word on each line.

2. A _____ is a social worker who works with foster children.

3. Lucy _____ around the corner timidly.

4. An education is _____ in order to get a job.

5. Duane used his _____ to buy a new skateboard.

6. My father was always _____ me of making the family late.

7. I was in the _____ of waking up early every Saturday and going for a five-mile run.

Write Sentences About the Story

◆ **Directions:** Use words from the story to answer these questions.

8. Why couldn't Sandra live with her own family?

_____

_____

9. When Sandra met Mr. and Mrs. Grove on their farm, why did Sandra just stare at them?

_____

_____

10. At the end of the story, why does Sandra say to Charlie, "You can call me Sandy"?

_____

_____

What's the Big Idea?

◆ 11. Which sentence tells what the whole story is about? Circle it.

    a. Foster children need special attention.

    b. Experiences help people to overcome their fears.

    c. Farms in the country are nurturing places.

Words and Meanings

◆ **Directions:** Think about how the **bold** words are used in the story. Then circle the answer that shows the meaning of each word or phrase.

12. Sandra decided that she wouldn't melt in the greenhouse, although **the air seemed sticky**. What does this mean?

    a. The air was moist and humid.

    b. The greenhouse was sticking to her.

    c. The air was dry.

13. He tried to **strike up a conversation** with her. This means he tried to _____.

    a. hit her

    b. talk to her

    c. avoid talking to her

14. Ray and Charlie went into the house to discuss the **books.** This means _____.

    a. the novels on Charlie's bookshelf

    b. the gardening books that Ray brought

    c. the accounting records

15. Her **heart was racing.** What does this mean?

    a. Her heart was beating slowly.

    b. She was having a heart attack.

    c. Her heart was beating very quickly from excitement or nervousness.

16. Charlie looked at Sandra, who returned his look with **pleading eyes.** What does this mean?

    a. She asked him to believe her.

    b. Her eyes gave the impression that she was asking him to believe her.

    c. She looked down at the ground and hoped he would believe her.

17. She felt like **a great weight was lifted from her shoulders.** What does this mean?

    a. She was relieved.

    b. She felt like she was being pushed down.

    c. She felt happy.

Letters and Sounds

◆ **Directions:** Though the following words are pronounced alike, they have different spellings and meanings. Read the words. Write them on the lines.

1. wear   _____

2. where   _____

3. ware   _____

> ▶ **TIP:** Words that are pronounced alike but have different spellings are called **homophones.**

◆ **Directions:** Read the words. Connect the words that sound alike.

4. herd	○ whether
5. stare	○ hare
6. air	○ border
7. hair	○ heir
8. weather	○ borne
9. boarder	○ heard
10. coarse	○ core
11. corps	○ stair
12. born	○ course

◆ **Directions:** Circle the word that correctly completes each sentence.

13. Her eyes met his with a cold (stair/stare).

14. He was (born/borne) in a log cabin.

15. (Where/Wear) are you going?

16. He was the (heir/air) to a large fortune.

17. She was going to the movies (weather/whether) he liked it or not.

18. They raised a (herd/heard) of cattle.

19. She was taking a chemistry (coarse/course) in college.

20. We crossed the (border/boarder) of Mexico.

Story Words

Directions: Read each word to yourself. Then say the word out loud. Write the word on the line. Check the box after each step.

21. America   Read ❑ Say ❑ Write ❑ _____
    (A | mer | i | ca)

22. democracy   Read ❑ Say ❑ Write ❑ _____
    (de | moc | ra | cy)

23. mansion (man | sion) Read ❑ Say ❑ Write ❑ _____

24. citizens (cit | i | zens) Read ❑ Say ❑ Write ❑ _____

25. supervise   Read ❑ Say ❑ Write ❑ _____
    (su | per | vise)

Word Bank

Write each of these story words in the Word Bank at the back of this book.

More Word Work

Directions: Many words are changed by adding a suffix such as **able, less,** or **ing.** The suffix **able** means "capable of" or "likely to." The suffix **less** means "without." Read the word. Write it on the line.

26. unbearable _____

27. thoughtless _____

28. declining _____

> **TIP:** Another word for a suffix is **affix.** In grammar, affix means a suffix or prefix added to a base word.

Directions: Write the word on the line. Circle the affix on each word.

29. comfortable _____

30. emotionless _____

31. understandable _____

32. unappealing _____

33. tireless _____

Use What You Know

This story is about Washington, D.C., the capital of the United States. What do you know about the capital? Write about it on the lines below.

_____

_____

_____

_____

OUR NATION'S CAPITAL

Washington, D.C., was designed to be a grand city. The details of its plan included broad avenues, public parks, historical monuments, and fine public buildings. It was designed to let the entire world know that America was here for the ages. The city's Greek and Roman style buildings **spoke** of America's beliefs of freedom and democracy, which started in those ancient cultures. Washington's creation was a sign of the beginning of a new nation. At the time of the first presidential election, Washington, D.C. had not yet been built. The United States did not have a capital of its own.

The swearing in of the first president of the United States took place in 1789 in New York City. Standing on Wall Street in downtown Manhattan, George Washington took the oath of office. It was a proud moment for the nation. Americans had survived years of the Revolutionary War and fought hard to win their long battle against England. It was now time to build a capital. To do this, Washington had to deal with two problems. One problem was paying off the country's debts from the war. The U.S. had not yet determined whether states or the new government would pay for its war debts. The other problem was to decide where to build the capital.

In the late 1700s, there were two very different ways of life in America. In the North, there were many cities. Banking and factory jobs were important. The South was mainly made up of farms and cotton plantations worked by slaves. The location of the capital was important to the North and the South, since both wanted the capital built in their own area. What is true of politics today was true of politics in President Washington's day. He knew that a compromise would be necessary. As a result, an agreement was made that the capital would be built in the South. The North would then have some of its war debts dropped.

Congress told Washington to select a place for the capital. It was to be no larger than ten square miles along the Potomac River. The President chose a spot where the Potomac and the Anacostia rivers meet. He named the area the District of Columbia after the explorer Christopher Columbus. This site was close to President Washington's home in Mount Vernon, Virginia. It was also a good spot for a seaport. This was important, since water travel was popular at that time.

Once the capital's location was decided upon, it was time to plan and build the city. A French engineer named Pierre L'Enfant was hired to complete the design. Washington, D.C., was one of the few cities planned before it was actually built. L'Enfant was thrilled to create an entirely new city.

He designed the city as a grid divided into four areas. The four areas of the grid were labeled for northwest (NW), northeast (NE), southeast (SE), and southwest (SW). Over this grid L'Enfant laid broad avenues that crossed each other at circular points. The highlight of the city would be the Capitol building at the city's eastern end. At the western end of the city would be the Mall where the Washington and Lincoln memorials are now located. In addition, the president's mansion, now called the White House, would have an important place. Throughout the city, L'Enfant planned circles and squares with small green parks. He wanted the city to be as beautiful as Paris in his French homeland.

L'Enfant was a talented but disagreeable man who angered many people. He would not give maps to city officials. He was afraid that before he could finish building his city, the land would be sold for profit. In fact, he took the lands of many rich and powerful men to build roads for the capital. Eventually, L'Enfant upset so many people that he was **fired.** A disappointed man, he took all his maps and plans with him. His two assistants replaced him. They were African American Benjamin Banneker and Irishman Andrew Ellicott. Between the two of them, they were able to put together L'Enfant's plans from memory.

Was the president's home always called the White House? Circle your answer.

Yes   No

Then keep reading to find out.

After the city's streets were planned, it was time to construct the buildings. The White House is probably the most famous building in Washington, D.C. The search for the person who would design the buildings began as a contest in newspapers across the country. The winner would receive $500 and the honor of designing the president's home. Many Americans believed the president's home should not look like a palace. The U.S. was a nation that had rejected kings and believed in the rule of the people. Americans wanted a home for their president that reflected this belief. But they also wanted the president to have a home where he would be proud to receive foreign officials. With this in mind, the simple and beautiful design of James Hoban was selected.

The building of the president's mansion began on October 13, 1792. It took many years to complete. President Washington never lived in it. After eight years of work, President John Adams and his wife, Abigail, became the first residents in November of 1800. Even after all that time, the house was still not completed. It was a cold place to live.

One year later, our third president, Thomas Jefferson, moved into the house. He was a man of fine tastes, and he began the task of decorating his new home. He wanted the best furnishings he could find. He ordered fine wallpaper and furniture from France. By 1801, most of the outside of the house was finished. It was the largest home in America.

During James Madison's presidency, the U.S. was once again at war with England. This was the War of 1812. In 1814, British troops attacked Washington, D.C. They set fire to the president's home. The First Lady, Dolley Madison, refused to leave the burning house. She insisted on rescuing the famous painting of George Washington. Because of her bravery, we still have this important painting. It is the only thing in the White House that was there when the house first opened. After the war, the damage to the house was repaired. However, the outside was still blackened by smoke marks. To cover the damage, the house was painted white. It was then that people began to call the president's house the White House.

The White House is the only private home of a head of state that is open to the public free of charge. In 1805, Thomas Jefferson held the first open house. It was a party to celebrate Jefferson's second presidential swearing-in ceremony. After his swearing in at the U.S. Capitol, the president greeted guests in the Blue Room. Jefferson also invited guests to the White House on New Year's Day and the Fourth of July.

In 1829, at the seventh presidential swearing in, President Andrew Jackson's celebration got a bit out of hand. Twenty thousand thoughtless guests tracked muddy boots through the White House. They stood on chairs and broke vases and lamps. Fearing for the president's safety, Jackson's aides moved him to a hotel. To get the guests out of the White House, the guards placed washtubs filled with orange juice and strong drink on the lawn.

By the time Grover Cleveland took office in the late 1800s, swearing-in crowds had become too large to bring to the White House. President Cleveland decided to set up a grandstand in front of the White House. Sitting in front of a large crowd, he watched the soldiers passing by. This practice has become a tradition of swearing-in parades. However, in 1993, President Bill Clinton brought back the tradition of inviting guests into the White House for a swearing-in party. That year 2,000 citizens were selected to be guests at the White House. The President, Mrs. Clinton, Vice President Gore, and Mrs. Gore greeted them.

Equally famous as the White House is the United States Capitol building. In addition to planning the city of Washington, L'Enfant was hired to design this building and to supervise its building. But L'Enfant refused to make any drawings for the building, saying that he carried the design in his head. This was one more reason why L'Enfant was fired.

The people still needed a Capitol, so another contest was held. Once again the prize was $500. The winner would design the Capitol that houses the Senate and the House of Representatives. A Scottish doctor named William Thornton won the contest. He designed a building made up of three sections. A low dome topped the center section. On each side were two rooms. One was to house the meeting chamber of the Senate. The other would house the meeting chamber of the Representatives.

The Capitol took many years to build. During the War of 1812, the English set fire not only to the White House but also to the Capitol building. If it were not for a sudden rainstorm, the Capitol would have burned to the ground. But once again, America defeated the English. The war was ended and repairs were made to the building. As the nation grew, so did the Capitol. Additions were made to the building. Soon steam heat, electricity, elevators, and air conditioning were added.

The Capitol building has been the home of Congress for over 200 years. Congress is made up of the Senate and the House of Representatives. This is the legislative branch of the government. The United States Constitution gives Congress the power to write the laws of our country. Elected by Americans, members of Congress write ideas for laws to the president. Before they officially become laws, these ideas are called "bills." The president, who makes up the executive branch of government, can do two things about a bill. If he likes the bill sent to him by Congress, he can sign it, making it a law. If the president does not like the bill, he can refuse to sign it. This is called a veto. If the president vetoes a bill, Congress can still pass it into law. After a revote, if at least two-thirds of Congress votes to pass the bill, it becomes a law. This is called overriding the president's veto.

The third branch of our government is the judicial branch. This is our federal court system. The highest court in our land is the Supreme Court. The judges of the federal courts review the laws passed by Congress. They make sure that the laws do not break any rules of the United States Constitution. If the judges believe that a law goes against the Constitution, they can reject it.

The founders of our country created the government so that no one branch would have too much power. The ability of one branch of government to undo the work of another branch is called checks and balances. The founders believed that this system would keep the government strong and the people free.

It took many years to build the nation's capital. At first, Washington, D.C., was a coarse, rugged town. In the early course of its history, it had many problems. Built on swampy land, it was full of mosquitoes. It was not a place where elected officials wanted to bring their families. There were few homes and the men lived in uncomfortable boardinghouses. Another problem was the slave trade. Washington was a port city and slave ships unloaded their human cargo daily. Foreign officials were disgusted by the terrible practice of selling human beings. The U.S. claimed to be a land of freedom and equality for all. However, it allowed slaves, who were without rights. This situation would haunt the city of Washington and the entire country until the Civil War.

Though there were many slaves in early Washington, D.C., there was also a group of free African Americans. Most of them lived in the northwest area of Washington in what is known today as Georgetown. Long ago, Georgetown's port handled large shipments of the area's tobacco crop. Most of the people worked in the warehouses and on the wharves along the waterfront. But a few famous African Americans lived there also. While helping Pierre L'Enfant to build Washington, D.C., Benjamin Banneker made the neighborhood his home. Another famous resident was Yarrow Mamout. This African American arrived in the U.S. as a slave. In spite of this, during the course of his long life he gained his freedom and owned his own home. He was one of the most popular figures in Georgetown. Another Georgetown success story was Joseph Moor. He also had been a slave. Like Mamout, Moor gained his freedom. An owner of a grocery store, Moor was a well-known and well-liked businessman.

Georgetown was safe for its free African-American residents, but they still faced problems. They were not allowed out on the streets after a certain hour at night. They were not allowed to walk together in groups of more than five or six. Even in church they faced unfair treatment. African-American members of a local church were not allowed to use the main stair to the church balcony. They were forced to enter the balcony by way of a separate stairway. Many churches forced their African-American members to sit in separate areas. Finally, in 1814, 125 African Americans in Georgetown formed their own church. Today it is the oldest African American church in Washington, D.C.

In addition to building their own churches, Georgetown's African Americans began to get schooling. They began by meeting in each other's homes to learn to read and write. In 1810, an English woman named Mary Billings opened the first school for African Americans in Georgetown. Her student, Henry Smothers, opened another school for the neighborhood's African-American children. In 1823, a church opened a school for both children and adults who wanted to learn to read and write. By 1827, a school for girls was opened by an African American woman named Maria Becraft.

Though there were bright spots like Georgetown in early Washington, D.C., the city was still a rough place. Because of its problems, visitors loved to poke fun at it.

Charles Dickens, the famous English writer, visited in 1842. He wrote that the city's large avenues started with nothing and led nowhere. He said that the mile-long streets had no houses and no people. Dickens claimed that the city felt like a **ghost town.** He wrote, "Such as it is, it is likely to remain." But Dickens was mistaken.

The U.S. had the vision to create a nation of laws based on freedom. The nation had the courage to move closer to the ideals that the country was founded upon. To celebrate those ideals, America created a beautiful capital for its citizens. Today, Washington, D.C., is a great city filled with government buildings, museums, theaters, businesses, homes, and parks. People come from all over the world to visit Washington and admire the beauty of America's capital.

You Be The Judge

◆ 1. Pierre L'Enfant was a talented but difficult man. Though his employers liked his designs for the capital, L'Enfant often angered them. Do you think L'Enfant should have been fired? Why or why not? Write what you think on the lines below.

_____

_____

_____

_____

Think About the Story

Use Story Words

◆ **Directions:** Look at your list of story words on page 152. Write a story word on each line.

2. The executive _____ is the home of the president and his family.

3. Pierre L'Enfant was hired to design and _____ the building of the new capital.

4. Americans believe in freedom and _____.

5. Foreign guests and American _____ visit Washington, D.C., every day.

6. The capital was built to celebrate _____ and its ideals.

When Did It Happen?

◆ 7. Write a number from 1 to 4 in front of each event to show when it happened.

_____ The Capitol building is finished.

_____ George Washington is elected president.

_____ President Washington selects a site for the new capital.

_____ The White House is set on fire.

What Were the Facts?

◆ 8. Why was Pierre L'Enfant fired? Circle the reasons.

a. He was late for work every day.

b. He took valuable land to build roads.

c. He didn't finish the White House on time.

d. He refused to provide maps or drawings to city officials.

Write Sentences About the Story

◆ **Directions:** Use words from the story to answer these questions.

9. When the White House was being built, what kind of home did Americans want for their president?

_____

_____

10. In 1814, when the British burned the White House, who saved the only object that survived the fire and what was it?

_____

_____

11. In its early stages, why was Washington, D.C., thought by some to be a coarse town?

_____

_____

_____

Words and Meanings

◆ **Directions:** Think about how the **bold** words are used in the story. Then circle the words that show the meaning of each word or phrase.

12. When the English writer Charles Dickens called Washington, D.C., a **ghost town,** he meant _____.
    a. it was full of cemeteries
    b. there were only a few people living there
    c. it was filled with ghosts

13. Pierre L'Enfant angered so many people that he was **fired.** To be fired means _____.
    a. L'Enfant got very angry
    b. L'Enfant was set on fire
    c. L'Enfant was let go from his job

14. When it was designed, Washington, D.C.'s buildings **spoke** of America's beliefs of freedom and democracy. Spoke means that it _____.
    a. sounded like a good place to live
    b. was a sign of the young country's beliefs
    c. was inspired by palaces in Europe

Letters and Sounds

◆ **Directions:** These words have the hard sound of **k** in **task.** Write the word on the line. Circle the letters that make the hard **k** sound.

1. mechanical _____   3. technical _____

2. unscheduled _____   4. chorus _____

◆ **Directions:** These words have the sound of **s** in **sun** or **sh** in **fish.** Write the word on the lines. Circle the letters that make the **s** or **sh** sound in each word.

5. scientists _____

6. parachute _____

◆ **Directions:** These words have the sound of **f** in **fish.** Write the word on the line. Circle the letters that make the **f** sound.

7. geography _____

8. physical _____

> **TIP:** The letters **ch** often make the **k** sound. Sometimes they make the **sh** sound. The letters **sc** can make the **s** sound when followed by **i** or **e.** The letters **ph** make the **f** sound.

◆ **Directions:** On the lines below, write the letter or letters for the sound that the underlined consonants make.

9. photogra<u>ph</u> _____   13. a<u>sc</u>end _____

10. <u>sc</u>ented _____   14. heada<u>ch</u>e _____

11. ar<u>ch</u>itect _____   15. al<u>ph</u>abet _____

12. ma<u>ch</u>ine _____   16. <u>ch</u>romosome _____

◆ **Directions:** Write letters on each line to correctly spell a word.

17. _____ ientific (**s** sound)   20. de _____ end (**s** sound)

18. tele _____ one (**f** sound)   21. Mi _____ igan (**sh** sound)

19. me _____ anic (**k** sound)   22. _____ antom (**f** sound)

Story Words

Word Bank

Write each of these story words in the Word Bank at the back of this book.

◆ **Directions:** Read each word to yourself. Then say the word out loud. Write the word on the line. Check the box after each step.

23. physicist   Read ❑ Say ❑ Write ❑ _____
    (phys│i│cist)

24. communications   Read ❑ Say ❑ Write ❑ _____
    (co│mu│ni│ca│tions)

25. simulations   Read ❑ Say ❑ Write ❑ _____
    (sim│u│la│tions)

26. mechanical   Read ❑ Say ❑ Write ❑ _____
    (me│chan│i│cal)

27. satellite (sa│tel│lite)   Read ❑ Say ❑ Write ❑ _____

28. engineer   Read ❑ Say ❑ Write ❑ _____
    (en│gi│neer)

29. external (ex│ter│nal) Read ❑ Say ❑ Write ❑ _____

30. weightlessness   Read ❑ Say ❑ Write ❑ _____
    (weight│less│ness)

More Word Work

You can use adverbs to describe verbs, adjectives, and other adverbs. Adverbs often tell **how**. They can also tell **where, why,** or **when.**

Examples: She could barely hear the voices over the engine's roar.
You must study very hard to be a successful scientist.
Her pillow is particularly soft.

◆ **Directions:** Write an adverb to describe each word.

31. landed _____   34. spoke _____

32. talked _____   35. laughed _____

33. walked _____   36. looked _____

▶ **TIP:** Many adverbs end with **ly.**

Use What You Know

Sally Ride was an astronaut on the space shuttle. Do you know of any space shuttle missions? What did they accomplish? Write what you know about a space mission on the lines below.

_____

_____

_____

_____

SALLY RIDE

"When you're getting ready to launch into space, you're sitting on a big explosion waiting to happen," says Sally Ride, the first American woman in space. For Ride, the launch was an exciting part of her space shuttle flight. She believes that space travel is different from any experience on Earth.

Ride was born on May 26, 1951, in Encino, California, near Los Angeles. Her father was a teacher at a college. Her mother was a teacher and counselor. Ride had several heroes while growing up. One was a high school teacher who encouraged her to study science. Early astronauts, such as John Glenn and Neil Armstrong, were also heroes. Her favorite subject in high school was math. She was also interested in astronomy and physical science.

As a child, Ride enjoyed sports. She was very good at tennis. She played at a national level and spent her weekends playing matches. After trying to play tennis as a pro, she decided that she was not good enough to continue as a professional tennis player. Instead, she went to Stanford University, where she earned degrees to become a physicist.

As Ride was finishing her studies in 1977, she read that NASA needed astronauts. Their job would be to conduct experiments in space. Ride decided that she wanted to see Earth from outer space, so she applied for the program. More than 8,000 people applied to NASA's space program that year.

Ride was tested and interviewed by experts at the Johnson Space Center in Houston, Texas. Afterwards, she returned home and awaited the results while finishing work on her Ph.D. in physics.

In 1978, she learned that she had been selected for the job at NASA. Of the 8,000 people to apply, only 35 were accepted for the program. Only six of those were women.

Ride had much training after she entered NASA. She learned many things. Among them were parachute jumping, water survival, radio communications, and navigation. She also had training in high-gravity and weightless environments. She had to learn all about the space shuttle, even though she would not fly it. Her training included flight simulations. These match space flight and help astronauts prepare for the actual mission. Ride enjoyed flying so much that she took lessons **on her own time** and became a pilot.

In 1979, Ride became an astronaut. This meant that she could be assigned to a space flight. Before going into space herself, she assisted on the ground with other space shuttle missions. As communications officer for flights of the space shuttle Columbia, she sent radio messages from mission control to the shuttle crews. Ride was expected to understand everything about a mission and stay calm no matter what happened. During this time, Ride also helped to design a mechanical arm for releasing and getting satellites in space.

In 1982, NASA chose Ride to serve as a crew member for the space shuttle's seventh mission. The flight needed a lot of preparation. She studied the flight manuals, step-by-step directions for every part of the flight, and practiced in the simulator. Computers make the simulator behave like an actual shuttle flight. Emergency situations are written into the computer's programs. This is done so that the crew learns how to handle the many things that might go wrong.

Ride became famous as she prepared to be America's first woman in space. Since she didn't want people to think she was chosen just because she was a woman, Ride disliked the attention and the many questions by reporters.

For her first space shuttle flight, Ride was given the job of flight engineer. This meant that she, the commander, and the copilot of the shuttle were responsible for the launch and re-entry of the shuttle. During takeoff and landing, she sat behind the commander and copilot. She helped them **to keep track of** thousands of dials and blinking lights on the control panel. During the flight, she and another astronaut conducted experiments. They also tested the new robotic arm.

There are three parts to the space shuttle. The part of the space shuttle that carries the astronauts is called the "orbiter." It is the part that has wings. The largest part of the shuttle is the external fuel tank. It is 18 stories high and 28 feet wide and holds the fuel used during liftoff. Solid rocket boosters are the third part of the shuttle. They are located on the sides of the external fuel tank and provide more power for liftoff. A lot of power is needed during liftoff for the space shuttle to escape the pull of Earth's gravity.

Ride and the Challenger crew took off from Kennedy Space Center in Cape Canaveral, Florida, on June 18, 1983. As the space shuttle took off, its engines roared and the shuttle vibrated. The noise was so loud that Ride could barely hear the voices from launch control through her headset. Ride is often asked if she was afraid during liftoff and the space flight. She says that there is no time to fear anything because a flight is so busy and exciting.

If you were an astronaut, how would you feel at liftoff? Write what you think on the lines below. Then keep reading to find out what takes place.

_____

_____

_____

_____

After two minutes, the solid rocket boosters had used up all of their fuel. They were released and dropped into the Atlantic Ocean. The orbiter became much quieter inside.

As the orbiter went up, Ride felt a great weight pushing against her chest and **pinning her to her seat.** This force was seven times greater than the force of normal gravity.

After eight and a half minutes, the external fuel tank was empty. It was later detached and burned up in space before it reached Earth. Smaller engines on the orbiter helped move the space shuttle into its orbiting position 184 miles from Earth. At that time, communication with the crew was switched to mission control in Houston, Texas.

Ride enjoyed the weightlessness of space travel. Astronauts floated from place to place in the orbiter. Ride even went to sleep while floating. She later enjoyed the view of Earth. The shuttle had windows that she could look through to see Earth and space. From the shuttle, she could actually observe cities and countries on Earth.

Challenger took 90 minutes to orbit Earth. It made 97 orbits. During the trip, Ride helped to launch satellites for other countries. The satellites weighed more than 7,000 pounds. During the next several days, Ride ran experiments. The experiments included work for companies and for schools. Ride and another crewmember, John Fabian, were the first astronauts to retrieve a satellite from space.

On board were 22 experiments created by high school and university students, a private company, and government groups. One of the experiments was created by high school students from Camden, New Jersey. It studied the effects of gravity and weightlessness on 150 carpenter ants.

When Ride was asked by mission control what it felt like to be up in space, she replied, "Have you ever been to Disneyland?" When the astronaut at Mission Control said yes, she said, "This is definitely an 'E' ticket." The more exciting rides at Disneyland once required a special "e-ticket" to ride.

Temperature in space ranges from minus 200 degrees Celsius to plus 200 degrees Celsius. However, inside the orbiter, the temperature remained between 70 and 75 degrees Fahrenheit. The astronauts wore light clothing, such as short-sleeved t-shirts and gym shorts.

From the window, Ride could see Oregon as they flew over Los Angeles and New York as they flew over Florida. She could see dust storms blowing over deserts and storms raging over the ocean. In space, she could see billions of lights from stars, planets, and other galaxies.

The astronauts were very busy almost all of the time they were in space. All of their activities were scheduled and controlled by NASA engineers.

The first satellite that Ride helped to release was the Anik C-2 communications satellite for Canada. This satellite would provide North America's first direct satellite-to-home pay-TV service. The release of the satellite marked the beginning of NASA's plan to use the space shuttle for profit work. This would earn NASA millions of dollars.

Ride took the controls. She watched the satellite spin in place at a rate of 50 spins per minute. The satellite would continue to spin when it was in place to keep it at its correct orbit. If the satellite didn't spin right, there was a chance the solar panels could melt. The astronauts felt a slight shake of the shuttle as the satellite was released from the cargo bay. Then they moved the orbiter away from the spinning satellite. It would take four days for the satellite to reach the planned orbit position.

The astronauts had to make changes to being weightless. Eating and cooking were tough. Floating pieces of food or water drops could cause the shuttle's equipment to break. Meals were cooked by two people and served in the shuttle's galley, or kitchen. The astronauts could choose from 25 different drinks and more than 75 kinds of food. A typical menu for a day included scrambled eggs, peaches, and orange drink for breakfast; hot dogs, almond crunch bars, bananas, and an apple drink for lunch; and shrimp cocktail, beef steak, broccoli au gratin, grape drink, and butterscotch pudding for dinner. Sticky foods like macaroni and cheese and peanut butter were easier to keep on a spoon.

The astronauts used a spoon and a pair of scissors to eat. They used the scissors to cut open the packages of food. They made the food by adding water into the package and waiting a few minutes for the food to mix. Some foods, such as ham, were cooked before the launch and reheated in a microwave. Nuts and cookies were kept in their original form.

The food packages were attached to trays. The astronauts strapped the trays to their legs or to tables that were mounted inside the shuttle. Sometimes they ate while floating! The astronauts usually ate together since it was more relaxing.

The crew had to make sure everything was completely clean when they finished eating. There was plenty of water on board. It was produced as a by-product by the fuel cells that made electricity for the shuttle.

The shuttle had bathrooms where Ride and the other astronauts could wash and brush their teeth.

Throughout the flight, the astronauts conducted the experiments on one another. They measured eye movements, vision, and more. With these tests, NASA hoped to solve space sickness, which affected many astronauts.

The astronauts did try to have some fun while in the orbiter. They had a race to see who could travel across the cabin the fastest. They pushed themselves off the wall in the direction they wanted to go. They also released a jar of jellybeans in the cabin. The jellybeans had been a gift from President Ronald Reagan. As the jellybeans floated around the cabin, the crew chased them and caught them in their mouths.

After six days in space, it was time to return to Earth. Because of weather conditions in Florida, the shuttle had to change its course and land in California. The commander, Robert Crippen, landed Challenger successfully at Edwards Air Force Base. Even though the landing was unscheduled, Ride had a small crowd of fans waiting for her.

Ride said of this flight, "The thing that I remember most about the flight is that it was fun. In fact, I'm sure it was the most fun I'll ever have in my life."

Ride went on her second mission in 1984. This time there was another woman on board, Kathryn Sullivan. She became the first woman to walk in space. Ride was a flight engineer for the mission again. This mission had a lot of problems. The first came when Ride tried to release a satellite. Two of the satellite's solar panels wouldn't open because the hinges were frozen. Ride solved the problem by using the robot arm to turn the satellite so that the sun could warm the hinges. Another problem was the loss of communications. However, the crew continued to work and solve problems as they arose. At the end of the eight-day mission, the shuttle landed safely at the Kennedy Space Center.

Ride's third flight into space was scheduled for 1986. However, her training was **put on hold** when Challenger exploded only minutes after liftoff for another mission. Everyone on board was killed. Ride was put on a special team to study the accident in Washington, D.C. The team found that the explosion was caused by a faulty part located on the solid rocket boosters. NASA has since changed the design.

Ride created NASA's Office of Exploration. She was also in charge of developing a long-range plan for future space travel. Her report on America's space program is known as the "Ride Report." The report recommended setting up a base on the moon. Scientists could then live and work in space at the same time. The report also suggested conducting a detailed look at Earth, using robots to explore space, and plans for a trip to Mars. While there are no plans to send people back to the moon, NASA is thinking about sending astronauts to Mars.

Ride had always wanted to return to Stanford University. She left NASA in 1987 to work for Stanford's Center for International Security and Arms Control. In 1989, she accepted a position as a physics professor at the University of California, San Diego. She also served for a short period as director of the California Space Institute. Another of her projects involved working with companies to develop products for space travel.

Her students may one day become astronauts and scientists. She shares her experiences with younger children as well. She has written several books for them about space and space travel. Her writing encourages students to follow their dreams. Ride also works to improve science education. She has received many awards for her efforts, including the National Spaceflight Medal. As Professor Ride, she enjoys her job at the University of California, San Diego. She does not want to give it up for more space travel. She enjoys teaching and finds it very rewarding.

Ride is an inspiration to many young people. Because of her hard work, she continues to serve as a role model for students interested in science and space travel. For students hoping to be scientists or astronauts, Ride has some advice. She believes the most important thing is to begin studying math and science in middle school. She encourages students to take an interest in an area of science, and then to work very hard. She believes there are many exciting careers in science for both men and women.

◆

You Be the Judge

◆ 1. If you had been in the NASA space program, would you ever have been ready to leave like Ride did? Write what you think on the lines below.

_____

_____

2. What do you think your favorite part of a space flight would be?

_____

_____

Think About the Story

Use Story Words

◆ **Directions:** Look at your list of story words on page 163. Write a story word on each line.

3. A _____ is someone who studies matter and energy.

4. Ride learned parachute jumping, water survival, radio _____, and navigation.

5. _____ are launched into space and used to communicate around the world.

6. Ride helped to design a _____ arm for releasing and retrieving satellites in space.

7. The largest part of the space shuttle is the _____ fuel tank.

8. When the conditions of space are imitated on Earth, these are called _____.

9. One kind of _____ drives a train; another is trained to work with science and technology.

10. Because there is no gravity in outer space, people experience _____ and can float in the air.

Write Sentences About the Story

◆ **Directions:** Use words from the story to answer these questions.

11. What did Ride do with NASA before she went into space?

_____

_____

12. What does it feel like when the space shuttle takes off?

_____

_____

Words and Meanings

◆ **Directions:** Think about how the **bold** words are used in the story. Then circle the words that show the meaning of each word or phrase.

13. Ride enjoyed flying so much that she took lessons **on her own time** and became a pilot. What does this mean?
    a. She told time differently from other people.
    b. The time when she was not at work.
    c. The time when she was working.

14. She helped **to keep track of** thousands of dials and blinking lights on the control panel. What does this mean?
    a. She helped watch and operate the control panel.
    b. She made pictures of all dials.
    c. She flew the space shuttle.

15. Ride felt a great weight pushing against her chest and **pinning her to her seat.** This means she was _____.
    a. held suspended over her seat
    b. turned upside down on her seat
    c. unable to rise from her seat

16. Ride's training was **put on hold.** This means _____.
    a. her training was delayed
    b. she held her training in her hand
    c. she continued her training

Chapter 3 Summary of Skills and Strategies

Let's look back at what you learned in Chapter 3.

Letters and Sounds

◆ You learned...

- ▸ the letters **ough, augh,** and **aw** can stand for the **aw** sound.
- ▸ the **or, ar,** and **ur** sounds.
- ▸ the different sounds for vowels combined with **r,** such as **or, ar, ir,** and **ur.**
- ▸ words with unusual spellings for the **k, s,** and **sh** sounds.

Stories and Skills

◆ You learned about...

- ▸ benefits and destructive powers of volcanoes.
- ▸ what happens to a girl and her new family when they make assumptions too rapidly.
- ▸ the early history of Washington, D.C.
- ▸ the first American woman in space.

◆ You learned...

- ▸ how to use what you know to help you understand stories.
- ▸ how to look ahead, or predict, what story characters might do.

Words and Meanings

◆ You learned...

- ▸ about the prefixes **mid, mis, sub,** and **trans.**
- ▸ about the suffixes **able, less,** and **ing.**
- ▸ about adverbs.

This chapter review will give you a chance to show what you have learned.

Part A

Summing It Up: Letters and Sounds

> ▶ The letters **ough, augh,** and **aw** can all stand for the **broad o** sound in **wrong.**

◆ **Directions:** Read each word. Circle the words that have the **aw** sound in **saw.**

1. pawn	4. laugh	7. fought	9. caught
2. tough	5. bought	8. lawn	10. rough
3. sought	6. taught		

◆ **Directions:** Write each word below on the lines. Circle the letters that stand for the **aw** sound.

11. pawn _____   15. lawn _____

12. sought _____   16. caught _____

13. bought _____   17. fought _____

14. taught _____

> ▶ The letters **ear** and **or** can stand for the sound of **ar** in **barn.**
>
> ▶ The letters **ear** and **ere** can stand for the sound of **ar** in **share.**
>
> ▶ The letters **ear** and **ere** can stand for the sound of **ir** in **irritate.**
>
> ▶ The letters **ear** and **or** can stand for the sound of **ur** in **fur.**

◆ **Directions:** These words have the sound of **or,** as in **fortunately.** Write the word on the line. Circle the letters that stand for the **or** sound.

18. fluoride _____   21. fluorish _____

19. coarse _____   22. boarder _____

20. fortune _____   23. important _____

◆ **Directions:** These words have the sound of **ar,** as in **part.** Write the word on the line. Circle the letters that stand for the **ar** sound.

24. harp _____   27. smart _____

25. carted _____   28. partner _____

26. heart _____   29. darted _____

◆ **Directions:** These words have the sound of **ar,** as in **care.** Write the word on the line. Circle the letters that stand for this **ar** sound.

30. wearable _____ 33. spare _____

31. paired _____ 34. hair _____

32. where _____ 35. there _____

◆ **Directions:** These words have the sound of **ir** as in **irregular.** Write the word on the line. Circle the letters that stand for this **ir** sound.

36. hemisphere _____ 39. hearing _____

37. tearfully _____ 40. fierce _____

38. pierce _____

◆ **Directions:** These words have the sound of **ur** as in **turbine.** Write the word on the line. Circle the letters that stand for this **ur** sound.

41. earnestly _____ 44. dirty _____

42. curb _____ 45. surfing _____

43. worthy _____ 46. learn _____

▲ ▸ Homophones are words that sound the same but have different spellings and meanings.
▲

◆ **Directions:** Read these words. Draw a line to match the words that sound the same.

47. hear ○ bare

48. stare ○ here

49. alter ○ altar

50. bear ○ stair

▲ ▸ The letters **ch** often have the sound of **k** in **task,** as in **technical.**
▲ ▸ The letters **ch** can also have the sound of **sh** in **fish,** as in **machine.**
▲ ▸ The letters **sc** can have the **s** sound in **sun** when they are followed by **i** or **e,** as in **scenery.**
▲ ▸ The letters **ph** have the sound of **f** in **fat,** as in **phonics.**
▲

◆ **Directions:** Read the words below. Write each word on a line under the word that has the same underlined sound.

chandelier	mechanism	ascent	scoreboard
scared	choral	rascal	charade
chute	chemist	science	descend

te<u>ch</u>nical		ma<u>ch</u>ine	
51. _____		54. _____	
52. _____		55. _____	
53. _____		56. _____	
<u>sc</u>enery		<u>sc</u>anner	
57. _____		60. _____	
58. _____		61. _____	
59. _____		62. _____	

Part B

Summing It Up: More Word Work

- ▶ A prefix is a word part that can be added to the beginning of some words to change their meanings.
- ▶ The prefix **mid** means "in a middle place or position."
- ▶ The prefix **mis** means "mistakenly or wrong."

◆ **Directions:** Read these words. Circle each word that has a prefix.

1. midnight
2. carpet
3. Saturday
4. misunderstood
5. midway
6. target
7. meaning
8. misinformed

Directions: Write on the lines each word you circled. Then write the prefix and base word that make it up.

9. _____ = _____ + _____

10. _____ = _____ + _____

11. _____ = _____ + _____

12. _____ = _____ + _____

> ▸ The prefix **trans** means "across or beyond."
> ▸ The prefix **sub** means "under."

Directions: Read these words. Circle each word that has a prefix.

13. subway   14. transplant   15. travel   16. substandard

Directions: Write each word you circled on the lines. Then write the prefix and the base word that make it up.

17. _____ = _____ + _____

18. _____ = _____ + _____

19. _____ = _____ + _____

> ▸ The suffix **able** means "capable of" or "likely to."
> ▸ The suffix **less** means "without."

Directions: Read these words. Circle each word that has a suffix.

20. breakable   21. pattern   22. careless   23. garbage

Directions: Write each word you circled on the lines. Then write the base word and suffix that make it up.

24. _____ = _____ + _____

25. _____ = _____ + _____

> ▸ Adverbs describe verbs, adjectives, and other adverbs.
> ▸ Adverbs can often tell how, where, why, or when.
> ▸ Many adverbs end in **ly.**

◆ **Directions:** Write an adverb on the line to describe each word that is **bold**.

26. The peanut butter was _____ **salty** for his taste.
27. He was late for school so he **ate** _____.
28. Because the problems were difficult, she did her math homework _____ **slowly**.
29. He was so distracted that he _____ **listened** to what his mother was saying.
30. Anne had practiced her speech and **spoke** _____ to the class.

Part C

Story Words

◆ **Directions:** On the lines below, write the word from the list that matches each clue.

volcano	ancient	benefit	necessary
electricity	destruction	caseworker	peered

1. something you can't do without _____

2. something that will help _____

3. very old _____

4. a break in the earth's surface _____

5. a power source that can be tamed _____

6. a kind of social worker _____

7. looked at intently _____

8. damage _____

Directions: On the lines below, write a word from the list to finish each sentence.

routine	accusing	democracy	supervise
allowance	citizens	mansion	America

9. They were _____ her of theft.

10. He always wanted to live in a _____.

11. His _____ was to do his homework before watching television.

12. The official name of our country is the United States of _____.

13. The U.S. government is a _____.

14. All _____ should vote.

15. It was her job to _____ the workers.

16. He wanted a raise in his _____.

Directions: On the lines below, write the word from the list that matches each clue.

physicist	mechanical	weightlessness	engineer
simulation	communications	external	satellites

17. defying gravity _____

18. not the real thing _____

19. made of machines _____

20. moons _____

21. a system for talking to others _____

22. on the outside _____

23. a person who plans or designs things _____

24. a student of the laws of nature _____

Part D

Think About the Stories

Fiction or Nonfiction?

◈ **Directions:** Write **fiction** next to the stories that were made up by the writer. Write **nonfiction** next to the stories that tell about real life.

1. "Lava Spill" _____

2. "Foster Child" _____

3. "Our Nation's Capital" _____

4. "Sally Ride" _____

Who Did What?

◈ **Directions:** Answer each question with the name of a person from the stories in Chapter 3.

Zeus	**Pierre L'Enfant**	**Ray**
Cynthia	**George Washington**	**Sandra**

5. Who remembers an eventful washing day on a Caribbean island?

   _____

6. Who was sworn in as president of the United States on Wall Street? _____

7. Who was sent to live in the country? _____

8. Who imprisoned Typhon under Mount Aetna?

   _____

9. Who was an accountant? _____

10. Who designed Washington, D.C.? _____

Why Did It Happen?

◆ **Directions:** Draw a line from each cause in Column A to its effect in Column B.

Column A	Column B
11. Because Sandra's friends were from the city,	○ Charlie sent him away.
12. Because Congress told him to,	○ President Washington chose a site for the capital.
13. Because Ray was stealing,	○ people are fascinated by them.
14. Because of the explosion of the Challenger,	○ he was fired.
15. Because Pierre L'Enfant refused to produce plans for the Capitol,	○ Sally Ride's training was put on hold.
16. Because volcanoes are powerful forces of nature,	○ her foster parents thought they were thieves.

Chapter 1 Story Words

◆ **Directions:** Write the words from the Story Words section of each lesson.

LESSON 1 ▶ **It's Never Too Late, Part 1**

_____

_____

_____

_____

_____

_____

LESSON 2 ▶ **It's Never Too Late, Part 2**

_____

_____

_____

_____

_____

LESSON 3 ▶ **Birthday Party**

_____

_____

_____

_____

_____

_____

WORD BANK

Chapter 1 Story Words, continued

LESSON 4   ▶ **Oprah Winfrey**

_____

_____

_____

_____

_____

LESSON 5   ▶ **Role Models**

_____

_____

_____

_____

_____

LESSON 6   ▶ **Against All Odds**

_____

_____

_____

_____

_____

Chapter 2 Story Words

◈ **Directions:** Write the words from the Story Words section of each lesson.

LESSON 1 ▶ **Finding New Friends, Part 1**

_____

_____

_____

_____

LESSON 2 ▶ **Finding New Friends, Part 2**

_____

_____

_____

_____

_____

LESSON 3 ▶ **Second Sight**

_____

_____

_____

_____

Chapter 2 Story Words, continued

LESSON 4 ▶ **Student Volunteer**

_____

_____

_____

_____

LESSON 5 ▶ **Blood Brothers, Part 1**

_____

_____

_____

_____

_____

LESSON 6 ▶ **Blood Brothers, Part 2**

_____

_____

_____

_____

Chapter 3 Story Words

◆ **Directions:** Write the words from the Story Words section of each lesson.

LESSON 1 ▶ **Lava Spill**

_____

_____

_____

_____

LESSON 2 ▶ **Foster Child**

_____

_____

_____

_____

_____

LESSON 3 ▶ **Our Nation's Capital**

_____

_____

_____

_____

_____

Chapter 3 Story Words, continued

LESSON 4 ▶ **Sally Ride**

_____

_____

_____

_____

_____

_____

_____

Notes

Notes

Notes

Notes